What's Wrong In America?

by

Arthur Siccan

This book was created in the United States of America

ISBN-13: 978-1-4818-46981
ISBN-10: 1-4818-46981

What's Wrong In America?

Table of Contents

Most chapters in this book start with a fictional account. All characters, except clearly identified historical figures, are fictitious. Any resemblance or similarity to actual people, either living or deceased, is purely coincidental. The fictional part ends at the double line ===============.

The fictional stories do not necessarily go to conclusion. It was not my intent to make the fictional parts the prime focus of this book, but rather to give a short story relevant to the main topic of the chapter to illustrate a theme. If enough of you let me know that you just must have "the rest of the story" perhaps that will be inspiration to write a full novel as my next project.

Preface

This is an anthology of essays addressing various issues, from the mundane to the vital. It is simply an expression of my observations and opinions. The reader may take these thoughts as an instigation of further thought, as a spark for introspection, or simply as the ravings of a disgruntled old man.

Before we go much further, let me explain that I love this country! Despite the negative or alarming tome of this work, I think this is still the greatest country to live in. What our Founding Fathers have established so many years ago, has endured, despite their fears and the result is astounding. We are so tremendously blessed with conditions in this country and the choices we can make, the freedom we enjoy. Yet, with time tends to come complacency, a lulling into security that may not be there.

With age comes experience, not necessarily in the sense of expertise, but simply as survival of the happenings of daily life. Needless to say, the expressions in these pages are the result of my experiences, factored, or biased if you will, by my personal beliefs. While many would consider me an educated man, having obtained a Master's Degree and worked in a professional capacity all of my career, I have no special training in politics, psychology, philosophy or other social specialties. My actions tend to be more on the organized, pre-planned and structured side rather than on the creative, artistic side. I am more of an engineer than an artist.

I am also what you might call a fundamentalist or traditionalist. I tend to prefer things as they are; that gives me a sense of stability and security. However, I definitely embrace new things if they are presented with good reasoning for their existence. I have actually frequently embraced new things as one of the early adopters. Also, in my profession I have often pioneered new techniques and methods.

Communications takes place by the sent message being processed, or filtered, through the sender's personality screen, and then, again, by the receiver's perception screen. I give you this overview of myself so that you can understand the filters through which these thoughts have been processed in my formulating them, just as you will process these thoughts through your perception screen.

I have given this book a different approach than most books. It is a combination of fiction and non-fiction. Each chapter starts with a fictional essay, followed by my thoughts and opinions regarding the real world. I have done this to put the subject into a more lively context, naturally dramatized for the novel appeal.

I hope that you will at least enjoy these ramblings, and I'd be pleased to no end if you will take these thoughts as a spark for your own thoughts on these topics. But, most of all, I pray that you have the courage to read these essays without fear and with an open mind. I say without fear because some of these topics will touch on your inner most being; some of these topics may give you a jolt as you contemplate whether the ideas presented have relevance to you. And, I say with an open mind because some of these topics will touch a hot button of yours that may be in conflict with my thoughts.

Have courage, be strong, and enjoy.

Arthur Siccan

Freedom & Liberty

The light appeared suddenly. He could only sense it through his eyelids; it must be very strong. It was so strong, as a matter of fact, that he dared not open his eyes. His mind was all fuzzy as he tried to remember where he was. The last thing that came slowly back from his memory was the bed on which he lay. He remembered that breathing was laborious and he was sure that he was going to die imminently. The day before, he had engaged Aaron Burr in a duel over Jefferson's election. He remembered the boat ride across the Hudson River to the New Jersey side, the palisades looming tall overhead.

Burr had asked for his support in his run for New York State Governor and re-nomination for Vice President. He remembered that he refused because he thought Burr was an unprincipled rogue. Consequently Burr challenged him to a duel. He detested duels but felt compelled to accept, lest he be labeled a coward. The image of the clearing on the bank of the Hudson was still crisp. It was early morning and the sun was already over the horizon on the New York side, casting an eerie light through the trees and bushes.

He can still hear his second, Nathaniel, shouting the word "Present". All time seemed to stand still as he turned to fire. But he had not intended to fire his pistol at all. Burr's bullet hit him in the chest and he dropped to the ground. The next thing he remembered was waking in his room, back in New York. That must be where he was now, but the light was too bright for that. It would be brighter than a sunlit day outside.

The monitors showed all points green. Dr. Peter Burr was pleased at the progress they were making. This is the third attempt and this time everything was going as expected. The first two attempts had been on unknown subjects; a man who had apparently died of cirrhosis of the liver and they had gotten special permission to use him as their first candidate for the Phoenix Project. They got as far as him opening his eyes, but then it went all wrong. Apparently the frequency setting had been calculated incorrectly. He relapsed into the world on the other side of the life/death boundary.

The second subject had been a young woman who had died in childbirth. They had been able to bring her back to life for a whole three weeks. After that, she complained of severe headaches all her waking hours. Pain killers and sedation were the only solutions they had. But even she returned to the other side.

It was a bit discouraging. It took almost two years for each subject. Taking samples of their DNA and then coming up with the right conditions to grow a clone. The growth process was very fast, creating a fully "adult" body and then slowing down to a normal aging rate. The greatest discovery came when he realized that he was able to rebuild the brain with the original's memories. In early cloning attempts, a clone was only identical to the original in physiological aspects. However, the learning had to start all over again, subject to the current environment. The clone looked the same, but it was a completely different individual. In this process, they wound up with a clone of the original body but all the memories and experiences of the original engrained in the clone's brain. The clone would for all intents and purposes be the original with a new body.

Dr. Burr had been nicknamed Frankenstein, after Mary Shelly's legendary scientist. He did not appreciate the nickname as that association was always in the context of horror and tragedy. Nobody dared call him Frankenstein to his face. Inwardly, though, he very much felt like the fictional scientist. The major difference was that he did not take body parts and stitched them back together. He started from scratch, taking only scrapings from the skull to get the DNA and remnants of the brain.

This time, they had gone back to the drawing board, so to speak, to review all their calculations and settings. Peter was absolutely certain that the process works. Getting a subject as old as Alexander Hamilton was the result of his friend Senator Mike Chilling. Mike was obsessed with bringing back a famous historical figure. Getting approval to use Hamilton was a miracle. But Chilling was good at convincing people to support his projects.

It was time to talk to the "patient" now that he showed signs of consciousness. Peter leaned close to the gurney and placed a gentle hand on Hamilton's arm. He felt a slight reaction to his touch. "Mr. Hamilton?" Peter said. "Please do not be alarmed. You are in good hands and your body is responding well to our treatments. How do you feel?"

"I'm very stiff but I can sense a bright light through my eyelids. My throat is dry, I could use a drink. But first, if you could please dim the lights, I'd like to open my eyes."

"Of course," Peter replied and motioned to an aide to turn down the lights.

He opened his eyes slowly, squinting to allow his pupils to adjust. As the room came into focus, he could see a white ceiling of some strange material he had never seen. It was textured somehow but basically flat and of a dimension he could not find plausible as there was no visible sign of support. What was holding it up, he wondered.

A nurse brought in a glass of apple juice and he drank it eagerly. As he raised his arm to bring the glass to his lips, he noticed a series of tubes connected to his arm and they seemed to penetrate right into his arm. He couldn't figure out what that was but it didn't hurt. And there were strange lines connected to his chest and his head. More mysteries.

Peter said: "Mr. Hamilton, you are in a special hospital. The next thing I'm going to tell you will seem impossible to you, but believe me, it is true. This is the year 2012. We have brought you back to life. Since your death, many things have changed, including science and medicine."

"2012? That is... that is... my goodness more than 200 years since I fought a duel with Aaron Burr. That is the last thing I remember."

"The irony of this situation, sir, is that my name is Peter Burr. My family tree does indeed trace back to your old nemesis. I hope that this will not place us at odds."

Alexander had some trouble assimilating all he had heard in the last few seconds. Where exactly was he? Was this still the United States of America? He had to know. "Are we still in the United States of America, sir? And is this still New York?"

Peter assured him that it certainly was. "But enough for now. I want you to get some rest while you are conscious. There is a lot for you to think about. We will have time enough to talk when you regain your strength in the coming days."

Peter was observing that Hamilton was remarkably alert and his biological functions all seemed in good order. This was encouraging indeed. But, he knew that it was much too early to think they were over the hump.

The following day, Hamilton was able to walk around unassisted. He decided to explore the hospital. Turning right, outside his room he passed other rooms, but their doors were closed. A bit further down the hall, he came to a wider space with a circular counter and several people behind it. He assumed that they were hospital staff. "Excuse me," he asked one of the women behind the counter.

"Oh, Mr. Hamilton, you should not leave your room unassisted," she replied.

"It's quite all right, my Dear. I feel fine and I must know where I am. I see so many strange objects all around me and such bright lighting all over the inside of this building."

"But Sir, ..."

"Tut tut," he cut her off. "Why don't you tell me what some of these things are around here? For example, that light box with pictures and writing in the window, what on earth is that?"

She glanced in his direction to understand what he meant by "light box" and noticed he was looking at the computer monitors on the nurses' station. "Oh, those are computers, eh... well, those are machines that can show things we have written, but only the writing is not on paper, but stored inside the computer. I don't exactly know how they work. Think of them as typewriters without paper."

She noticed a puzzled expression on his face and realized that he wouldn't even have seen a typewriter yet. "Come on around to this side and let me show you," she motioned him to come around the end of the counter. She explained to him that one pushes on the little buttons on the keyboard and as she demonstrated, words appeared on the screen.

"I can write whatever I want and it is stored inside the computer. I can erase things if I no longer need them or make a mistake. I can also capture pictures and store them."

"But, the pictures are so real, not at all like a painting. How did you create those?"

"We have cameras that can capture a real life image of what they 'see' and then store those as well. Here, let me show you." She sat down in front of her monitor and activated her camera. As she moved her head, the image on the monitor moved accordingly. Hamilton was fascinated as he witnessed this miracle. It was spooky to him. She clicked on a "button" on the screen and the image stopped moving. "I just took a snapshot of my image and it is now a picture that I can save inside the computer and later use it."

Hamilton's head began to swim but he had to believe his eyes. He'd always been a person to grasp things quickly and thus he absorbed what she explained in his limited capacity to try to categorize these new experiences as best he could. But when she said that she could send the words and pictures to someone else that was not even in the room, he could not understand what she was saying, so he left it for now. One lingering thought stayed with him though as he returned to his room. The nurse had said she could erase things she'd "written". That certainly would have been useful in drafting the Declaration and the Constitution.

The following day, he spoke with Dr. Burr. He still had a spooky feeling about his name, realizing that he was a direct descendent of his killer. He wanted to know everything that has changed in the last 200 years, he told him. Peter chuckled and said: "That will take more than a few days, but we can begin. I will arrange for George Williams to take you around and show you things. He can explain anything that is strange to you and I'm sure that will be a lot."

"That would be very kind of you. Thank you!"

The next several days, Hamilton spent with Williams and he just could not stop being amazed at the incredible things and images he saw. The streets were paved with a solid, smooth material and there were many vehicles rolling along, under their own power because there was not a horse in sight. The buildings were impossibly tall and they had huge windows with glass in them; some of them looked like they were made completely of glass.

Hamilton had a sudden desire to see his grave site. Williams said: "OK, let's go there." When Williams tried to take him down some steps into a hole in the sidewalk, he hesitated. "It's quite all right, Alex. This is what we call a subway. It's a bit noisy when the train comes, but you will be quite safe."

His curiosity gave him the courage to follow Williams down into the hole. He was amazed when he saw the train gliding along on two smooth metal bands down in a pit that went into the distance inside a dark tunnel in both directions. He could see that the means of illumination made this possible. Without the light, he could not see how people could live and move underground. He was afraid to ask how the tunnels were created in the first place.

"Is Washington still the capital of America?" he asked as they rode the subway downtown.

"Yes it is, has been since we first set it up. I'm sure you'll have an opportunity to see it soon. Needless to say, you'll not recognize it."

Hamilton suddenly became aware of numerous black people on the train, who seemed to behave like the white people. They did not act like slaves. He leaned close to Williams and asked: "I'm just wondering, all the black people here around us, are they slaves or have we finally come to our senses and set them free?"

Williams explained to him that in 1865 the Civil War was won by the North and slavery was officially abolished. Hamilton bowed his head and he could not help himself, but tears welled up in his eyes. *Oh glorious God, I thank you that your will has prevailed. Thank you, thank you, thank you!* he prayed. Williams noticed the change that came over Hamilton and stole a sidelong glance at him but he left him to his thoughts.

They arrived at Rector Street station and made their way back above ground. Williams took him up Rector Street along the graveyard that surrounded Trinity Church. As they came almost up to Broadway, he nudged Hamilton and nodded his head towards a rather prominent grave marker with a slender pyramid atop. Hamilton followed his eyes and saw the name Hamilton on the monument. "That's mine?" he asked. Williams nodded is head in confirmation.

They made their way around to Broadway, to the front of Trinity Church and Hamilton had to hold his breath at the sight of the church. It had been a rather modest structure in his time. Apparently it had been rebuilt. They then walked up close to his grave. He noticed that the dirt around the monument seemed to have been recently repaired and then it struck him. Of course, they had to dig up his body. That thought did not cheer him up. After 200 years, there wasn't much left of his body, he would think. That will be more questions for Dr. Burr.

He looked at his grave marker, which was way too large for his liking. It was embarrassing. He blushed as he read the inscription:

"TO THE MEMORY OF
ALEXANDER HAMILTON
The CORPORATION OF TRINITY CHURCH Has erected this
MONUMENT
In Testimony of their Respect
FOR
The PATRIOT of incorruptible INTEGRITY
The SOLDIER of approved VALOUR
The STATESMAN of consummate WISDOM
Whose TALENTS and VIRTUES will be admired
BY
Grateful Posterity
Long after this MARBLE shall have mouldered into
DUST
He died July 12th 1804, Aged 47"

"Hmmm, this is embarrassing," he told Williams. "I mean, I'm glad people of the time appreciated my efforts, but this is a bit over the top."

Williams said to him with a broad smile on his face:

"Wait 'til you see the statues."

"No, thank you, we'll do without that, if you please. What I would like to do is gather up some newspapers and just sit and read what's going on. Is the *New York Post* still around?"

"It sure is, we'll pick up a copy. But we'll grab several newspapers. You'll have plenty to read."

The following day, Hamilton read the newspapers front to back and was amazed. He was curious about all the advertisements that occupied more space than the stories. He must ask Williams about that.

As he was reading, he was getting an unsettled feeling though. There were articles about murders, rapes, people having issues with young people praying on a playing field, separation of church and state, people being arrested by police at public gatherings. His mind was spinning. There was news about reducing Social Security and Medicare, whatever those were. It seemed people were getting money back from the government; strange indeed. He must talk with Williams about that as well.

Hamilton's mind was seriously agitated. He didn't like what he was reading at all, even though he didn't understand all of the technology. It seemed to him that things had gone terribly wrong in this country over the last 200 years. He could hardly wait to speak with Williams about these matters. But Williams had been called out of town and Dr. Burr was too busy as well. It would just have to wait.

Finally, after three days, Williams came to visit Hamilton to see how he was doing. "George, I am doing well, kind of, but I am very confused and agitated about what I've read in the papers. Can we spend some time to talk?"

"Sure, I'm free this afternoon, if you like," Williams replied.

That afternoon, Hamilton went to Williams' office and they settled in for their chat. Hamilton had a stack of articles from the papers in his hands, many marked up with a pen to highlight sections of text.

"I don't know where to begin, I have so many questions. Hmmmm. let's start with the role of government, the federal government specifically. These things called Social Security and Medicare seem to be handouts from the feds, as you call them now. What is that all about?"

Williams had to think for a moment and then said: "Social Security is a fund of money that working people contributed to over their working life, a percentage of their income. Their employers also contributed into this fund. When they retire at the end of their working life, they get money out of that account to help them with their expenses. Think of it as a retirement savings account run by the government."

"And why is the federal government involved in this? Couldn't the people just save money in a bank for their retirement?"

"They could and they can. However, back in 1935, under President Franklin Roosevelt, the feds decided that there were too many old people, widows and orphans that had no income and economic times were bad. Under Roosevelt's guidance, they feds decided to establish a country-wide, equally accessible program to provide this retirement insurance. Initially it was just provided to people of certain professions. Only later it was changed to cover essentially everybody."

"Fascinating," Hamilton observed, "but, isn't that rather a bit socialist? I mean, even the name 'social security' points to that. In my earlier time, this concept had just been identified by the Frenchman Henri de Saint-Simon. You mean to tell me then that this concept took hold in this country?"

"I suppose so. There were many who objected to creation of the Social Security system, but the feds prevailed. It is a great burden on our society because the demographics are changing. When you have a system like this, where the working people provide the funds for the beneficiaries and the number of working people compared to retired people changes, the money is not really there."

Hamilton couldn't believe his ears. "You mean the money retired people get isn't just the money they put into the system? You mean it's not like an individual retirement savings account where my specific contributions are what is paid back to me?"

"That's right, think of it as a savings pool."

"Wow!" Is all Hamilton could say. "So, what about this Medicare thing?"

Williams tried to explain: "That is somewhat similar to Social Security except it is insurance for medical expenses only. Working people also pay into this fund and after they retire Medicare pays most of their medical expenses."

"You know, George, one of the things we worried about a lot when we framed the Constitution, was the size and power of a federal government. We were convinced that a government that grew too powerful would be a threat to individual liberties. We got a lot of objections from the Antifederalists over this. We had hoped that by spelling out the specific powers of the federal government we had it covered.

"Yet here we now have a government that is in the thick of things like individuals' insurance. That is what we considered a commercial issue and never dreamed that the government would get into that. But is seems to me that people, especially retired people are at the mercy of the government. That scares the living daylight out of me."

Williams could see the agitation in Hamilton's mind. He was trying to remember what he had read about the Founding Fathers and the creation of America. He felt sorry for him.

"Let's talk about this prayer in public thing. I see there are several cases where a bunch of baseball players, and I saw that is a ball game being played these days," Hamilton said with a smile, "knelt down to pray on the field before and after their game. And then some individual was upset over that and brought a lawsuit against the team to try to stop them from doing that. Please tell me, George, that this isn't really true."

With a heavy sigh Williams explained: "There are those in this country who think that expression of religious faith in public and on public lands is inappropriate."

Hamilton's eyes became moist as he contemplated this development. "And then there is this article about thousands of people gathering here in New York, down near Wall Street, protesting some issue with the wealthy people yet police came along and made them disburse. Surely that must be a mistake."

Again, Williams tried to frame his response gently. "Local governments have decided that they need to control the gatherings of crowds on the basis of safety and health issues. Many localities require a permit to gather in large crowds for that reason."

"Oh God, it's King George III all over again. I had such high hopes that we had found the right solution to prevent this from reoccurring. If people need a permit to gather, then it's not a right any more as the permit could be denied. Consequently, gatherings are now at the whim and leisure of the government. Dammit, that is in direct violation of the Constitution. I'm sorry for my outburst, but this is too much."

He broke down crying, heavy sobs wracking his whole body, tears streaming down his cheeks. "Oh why, oh why did you bring me back? I wish I'd been left alone in my death. This is too painful to bear."

=====================

You've heard or seen the phrase: "Freedom is not free!" You'd think that people would do whatever it takes to maintain freedom and protect our liberties and rights. Curiously this is not happening. Actually there are those in America who would do whatever it takes to eliminate your rights and curtail your freedom. And the scary part is that they are the ones who are in power. Yes, I'm talking about our government leaders who run the federal, state and local governments. The America that our Founding Fathers created is no longer. The government of three branches has been eclipsed by the fourth branch: the administrative branch.

Let us pause, for a moment, to contemplate why we experience fear and pain. My purpose will be clear in a moment. Are they instilled in us to help us survive? Or, have we survived because they have been instilled in us? Either way, when the body experiences pain, it knows to react in the proper way that will prevent further damage to the body. When we experience fear, it is fear of a real or imagined threat. In any case, it alerts our brain to take appropriate action that will eliminate or circumvent the threat.

I bring this up because this chapter and the one on Big Brother, should instill fear in you and motivate you into action.. Unfortunately, we are like the frog that is placed in a cold pot of water which is heated slowly, slowly to the boiling point. Each extra degree of heat is hardly noticeable or at least the frog thinks "Hmmm, that isn't too bad, I can handle this." Alas, what is happening to us in America is hardly noticeable. With each small infringement of our rights we seem to say: "That's not too bad, we can handle this." That is why it is so insidious.

In case you have not noticed, it is human nature to grab more and more power. Power is intoxicating; it goes to the head of those who have it. Our Founding Fathers knew this. But let us go back to the beginning, or close to it. John L. Hancock does a wonderful job in his book *Liberty Inherited* (available on Amazon) describing the origin of our liberties and rights. Therein he traces the background of the Founding Fathers and the beliefs they had inherited from their ancestors. As he goes into some detail, he points out that at the time of the American Revolution, all other countries, in particular European countries, were monarchies or dictatorships, where individual people had no rights but rather served a select few elites. The concept of a people being ruled by a government that serves the people, at the leisure of the people, was totally foreign. Hancock maintains that the creation of a country like the United States of America under these circumstances was nothing short of a miracle.

The essence of what America is and what it means to be an American is a certain, unshakable belief that all men are created equal and support a limited government, individual rights (vs. state rights), the sanctity of private property and free market economics. This essence was the driving force in drafting the Declaration of Independence and later the Constitution of the United States. This whole belief system, as Hancock points out in his book, originated in England many years before the Declaration of Independence. The English people had shaken off the shackles of a ruling monarchy with absolute rights over the people in 1688 and established a government where individual rights, a limited government, private property and free market economics became the accepted law of the land. No other country was willing to follow this path at the time. The success of that form of government is attested to by the many nations emulating a representative democracy.

When the pilgrims came to the colonies, they brought this spirit of freedom and liberties with them. It became a core part of their beliefs and behaviors. The colonies of Spain and France, on the other hand, did not benefit from this history. So, as Hancock points out, America could only spring from the English colonies, where the seeds of freedom were planted, albeit in shallow soil.

With the establishment of America and its unique form

of government, a series of events were set in motion that had global impacts, without exaggeration. America became the strongest nation in the world and a role model for other nations who were forming or reforming their government. This lasted into the early part of the twentieth century. Up to that time, the original American spirit was alive and well as evidenced by the belief in individual rights, sanctity of private property and the free market economic system. You could see this spirit on the frontier as well as in the cities.

At the founding, America was to be a nation where government is believed for the first time to embrace the high purpose of defending the equal rights of every citizen and that no man may be rightly governed except by his consent.

The sad thing is that in the last nine decades or so, the American people have been sold a bill of goods which we have swallowed hook, line and sinker. That bill of goods is the concept that the government will take care of you, that private property is not as important as the needs of developers, that markets need to be regulated and controlled, business decisions are best controlled by the government via tax rules and incentives, the government can tell you what you must buy, that the government needs to grow to take care of all the governing needs and increasing bureaucracy, the right to defend yourself is subjugated to the criminal's protection from unusual punishment, and even that all men do NOT have equal rights, just to name some examples.

We have allowed the government to create a fourth branch of government: The Administrative Branch. This is the "branch" of government that is not elected, answers only to Congress and the President and is allowed to make regulations (in effect laws) without due legislative process, not to mention total lack of representation. Defenders of the administrative branch claim it is the only effective way to protect our individual rights as well as our political and social mores.

Larry P. Arnn, President of Hillsdale College addresses

this administrative branch further in his book *The Founders' Key*.

"Many events, including the Great Depression, revealed to the new Progressive thinkers that through the evolution of time, there is evolution of rights. Unless we keep up with that evolution, and even begin to shape that evolution, we will be overcome and lose all rights. It is the job of government, they believe, to protect equality though new measures to guarantee that the results of economic competition do not get out of hand.

"It had to be this way, argue the new thinkers, because times have changed. It is the way of times to change and the Founders were wrong to think they do not. The kind of government they built is not adaptable to the new circumstances, so we have to change it. In particular, we have to organize government to be more active in more ways, and also it must be more scientifically based. In fact, we have to invent a new branch of government system, the ... "fourth branch" ... This new branch will be able to perform all kinds of wonderful things because of its training. Also, it will be wholly focused on the public good because it will operate quite outside the politics and beyond political control, and also because its members will be safe in their jobs. ... They will get along with one another very well because they will run a unified system: legislative, executive, and judicial powers will be rolled into a single agency.

"This is the origin of the entitlement sate and the administrative system that goes with it. Built on a different understanding of nature, equality, and of consent, it proposes different policies and different ways of pursuing them. It sets out to solve the problems of want, misfortune, and injustice in the society. It holds out the great hope of a planned and rational society, in which none need suffer unduly and all who suffer will have relief. These are the new self-evident truths it has discovered.

What Dr. Arnn describes here is the basis for our current state of affairs. An America that has slipped from a representative democracy and capitalist economy to a form of socialism. The government will control all and take care of all.

The following list continues to illustrate how we've turned this country upside down. You know you live in an Upside-down Land if...

- Politicians think that stripping away the amendments to the constitution is really protecting the rights of the people.
- The rights of the Government come before the rights of the individual.
- The equal rights to life, liberty and the pursuit of happiness have been redefined as equal rights to the production of others, such as government entitlements distributed by group rather than merit.
- Wealth is redistributed by the government in stead of by the effort of individuals.
- Murderers and rapists are given relatively light prison sentences that are served in prisons with many of the comforts of outside life and then are likely commuted to shorter terms or parole.
- You can get arrested for expired tags on your car but not for being in the country illegally.
- Your government believes that the best way to eradicate trillions of dollars of debt is to spend trillions more of our money.
- A seven year old boy can be thrown out of school for calling his teacher "cute" but hosting a sexual

exploration or diversity class in grade school is perfectly acceptable.

- The Supreme Court of the United States can rule that lower courts cannot display the 10 Commandments in their courtroom, while sitting in front of a display of the 10 Commandments.
- Children are forcibly removed from parents who appropriately discipline them while children of "underprivileged" drug addicts are left to rot in filth infested cesspools.
- Working class Americans pay for their own health care (and the health care of everyone else) while unmarried women are free to have child after child on the "State's" dime while never being held responsible for their own choices.
- Hard work and success are rewarded with higher taxes and government intrusion, while slothful, lazy behavior is rewarded with EBT cards, WIC checks, Medicaid and subsidized housing.
- The government's plan for getting people back to work is to provide 99 weeks of unemployment checks (to not work).
- Being self-sufficient is considered a threat to the government.
- Parents believe the State is responsible for providing for their children.
- You can compile a book like this just by reading the news headlines.
- You pay your mortgage faithfully, denying yourself the newest big screen TV while your neighbor defaults on his mortgage (while buying iphones, TV's and new cars) and the government forgives his debt and reduces his mortgage (with your tax dollars).

- Your government can add anything they want to your kid's water (fluoride, chlorine, etc.) but you are not allowed to give them raw milk.
- Being stripped of the ability to defend yourself makes you "safe".
- You have to have your parents signature to go on a school field trip but not to get an abortion.
- An 80 year old woman can be stripped searched by the TSA but a Muslim woman in a burqa is only subject to having her neck and head searched.
- When asked where specifically does the Constitution grant Congress the authority to enact an individual health insurance mandate, the Speaker of the House (Nancy Pelosi) responds: "Are you serious? Are you serious?"

If you're starting to get discouraged about the sad state of affairs in America by now, you should. We have succumbed to that bill of goods our politicians have sold us, a little at a time, as we continue to watch TV, play computer games, pursue various entertainment, collect our government handouts, avoid the voting booth because it's too much work to protect our freedom. We don't take our representatives to task for not representing our wishes. We give up without trying because we think it won't make any difference. And it's going to get worse...see the chapter under "Big Brother."

But, before we leave this topic, let us look at the structure of our government. We call it a democracy. However, there are two types of democracy: a *direct democracy* and a *representative democracy*. In the direct democracy, every citizen has direct involvement in the decisions of the government. In a representative democracy, the individual citizens exercise their wishes in the governing decisions through their elected representatives. When America was formed, it was decided to make it a representative democracy. The reasons were a matter of practicality. America was huge, distances between the seat of government and the citizens were many hundreds of miles in many cases. It was simply not practical to bring all citizens together to make decisions.

We have survived with this method of government to this day, but not very well. Our legislators churn out laws every day on subjects as diverse as healthcare and immigration and registrations, licenses, fees, taxes, minority business requirements, environmental issues, and on and on. Often the laws that are passed are those desired by the most vocal individuals that can manage to get access to their representatives or those who pay the most money in political support. The mass of legislation has become so huge that it boggles the imagination how our representatives can even cope with it.

In *The Federalist* James Madison made reference to the complexity of laws:

> "It will be of little avail to the people, that the laws are made by men of their own choice, if the laws be so voluminous that they cannot be read, or so incoherent that they cannot be understood; if they be repealed or revised before they are promulgated, or undergo such incessant changes that no man, who knows what the law is do-day, can guess what it will be to-morrow. Law is defined to be a rule of action; but how can that be a rule, which is little known and less fixed?"

In their significant wisdom, our Founding Fathers knew very well what lay ahead and what the perils of our new government would be. I'm afraid we have lived up to their worst fears.

As a nation we have not yet grasped that we can get closer to a direct democracy than ever before. Current technology would allow us to partake more directly in the governing process. But those in power apparently don't want to share in this governing process. An example is the proposition process where a particular measure passes the test of sufficient interest via collected signatures that support a measure to appear on the regular voting ballot. Here is a perfect example of the people expressing their wishes on a particular issue. Yet, even with overwhelming passage by votes of a proposition, our judges review the issue and decide whether it's legal or not, never mind the wishes of the people.

One famous (or infamous, depending on your point of view) example is Proposition 8 in California. This measure attempted to define marriage as the union of one man and one woman. It was passed in the voting booth by a significant majority. The people of California had spoken and expressed their wishes. This was a clear example of democracy (even direct democracy) in action. However, our politicians and judges, aided of course by a team of lawyers, decided that the will of the people was not important. It is not my intent in this passage to debate the pros and cons of Proposition 8 or what should constitute the definition of marriage, but rather to point out that in a true democracy, direct or representative, the will clearly expressed by the majority of a people should govern. Anything else will lead to anarchy.

Another significant surrender of our individual rights is our election process. Abraham Lincoln, in his Gettysburg Address, summed up the intent of the Constitution thusly: "That government of the people, by the people and for the people shall not perish from the earth." And yet, after so many men fought and gave their lives in the Civil War, what have we done to ourselves? We have let institutions take over the decision making process by which our representatives and presidents be elected. We have allowed labor unions and corporations to promote political campaigns.

One of the significant milestones that promoted the ability of organizations to conduct such political actions is the Supreme Court's ruling in *Citizens United vs. Federal Election Commission* in 2010. The Court's ruling confirmed that corporations and labor unions would be allowed to spend their money on political expenditures due to the First Amendment [of the Constitution] guaranteeing individuals the right to free speech. In other words, we have allowed the Supreme Court to confer the status of individuals to organizations. Am I the only one shaking his head in disbelief here? Organizations are clearly not individuals; they are groups of individuals governed by a few individuals in a pure business (read dictatorship) environment. The members or employees have no democratic say about how the organization shall conduct itself, i.e. in political actions.

I suspect that you can readily see that the clout of an organization to present a polarized message is far greater than the clout of the individuals who make up that organization.

At the beginning of this chapter (the non-fiction part) I hinted that you might be afraid, which should motivate you into action. So, if you're feeling a bit uncomfortable or concerned about the fate of democracy, freedom and liberty in this country, you owe it to yourself to read John Hancock's *Liberty Inherited*. He concludes with suggestions of what you can do to preserve the American ideal so that your children and grandchildren can rest assured that limited government, individual rights, private property and free market economics will prevail, not only in America, but throughout the world.

At he very least, I hope you will make yourself familiar with the Declaration and the Constitution. The next thing we all need to do is take an active interest in the laws being formulated and then engaging our representatives. They are easily reached on the internet.

If you have an interest in a better understanding of the Declaration and the Constitution, Hillsdale College is conducting a nationwide education campaign on those documents and American liberty for free.

BIG BROTHER

Big Brother

It was a hot day again but fortunately the park had shade trees. The grass was a lush green due to the profuse sprinkling. He wondered how they could justify the huge amounts of water required for keeping the grass so green in this desert. Las Vegas at least had the sense to use desert landscaping, which consisted mostly of gravel and drought tolerant plants, certainly no grass.

Anyway, Hugo was counting the number of people that showed up as the time for the rally neared. About 300 had RSVP'd and it looked like word of mouth has brought out more than that.

"Hey, let's go and take our position under that big elm," he nudged his friend Saul. "The shade will be in the right place as the sun moves across the sky."

Saul gave him a curt nod and slowly got to his feet. This was going to be a meeting to discuss the many liberties that we have lost since the founding of America. Here we were in the year 2048, and you wouldn't recognize this country any more. When you read the history, like Thomas Paine's *Common Sense* the *Federalist Papers* and the

Antifederalist Papers, not to mention the Constitution of the United States and the Declaration of Independence, you just wound up shaking your head in sorrow and wonder how we got to this point.

Getting a hold of these documents was a trick to be sure. The feds had removed all access to these documents on the internet. Paper copies had been lost over the years long ago as the world turned to a "paperless" society. Hugo had a paper copy of all four documents and he had scanned them into his computer while he was off-line; he unplugged the cable from his Ethernet port to make sure and he never used wireless. That was an open invitation for the feds to snoop on your activity.

He set up a phony account so that he could e-mail it to his friends, who had similar illegal phony accounts. Thank God for the hackers that could still provide the untrackable accounts. Of course if they ever did connect you with one of those, it meant a minimum 1-year prison term. But Hugo had always been one to live on the edge of the law. He'd been lucky so far.

Today's discussion was sure to be monitored by the Peacekeepers ("Peacers" for short), as the local police had come to be called. That term had gone nationwide as city after city adopted the euphemism. Peace was about the last thing they kept as they enforced the laws according to their own interpretation. Their existence would soon change as well, though, Hugo was certain. There was pressure being exerted on the localities to hand the nation's "peacekeeping", i.e. police actions, over to a federal force. He thought it would likely become an extension of the military.

So, even though the Constitution was hard to come by, it was still officially in effect. The Supreme Court, backed by President Woolings, was making every effort to suppress that glorious document by interpreting its meaning as the Court saw fit. Good old Woodrow Wilson had started the movement back near the beginning of the twentieth century, by declaring that a document like the Constitution had to adapt to the changing situations of a nation; that it can't be cast in concrete. Apparently, the basic rights of life, liberty and the pursuit of happiness were subject to interpretation.

What this means is that officially we still had a right to "peaceably assemble". However, the local authorities were worried about the impact of large gatherings on their precious landscaping. So, they tried to impose a permit requirement for any gatherings. Well, it doesn't take a political science degree or a law degree to figure out that any permit is essentially an infringement on the right to assemble. A required permit implies that the permit might not be granted, and that is a denial of the right to assemble, regardless of the reason.

Needless to say, we did not apply for a permit. We were going to take a stand against this infringement. It was a heated situation to be sure; it might even be a powder keg. Hugo again felt for his Colt 87 in the back of his belt. It was a sweet weapon for close-up combat. The laser sight made it a cinch to target and let loose. The built-in gyro helped keep it steady and on target for repeat shots, but it also made it just a bit sluggish to change target. An adept user could activate and deactivate the gyro with his thumb and realign the gun very quickly.

He hoped it would not come to that, but he was determined not to let the Peacekeepers get the upper hand. He was convinced that every other attendee at this rally had a similar gun with them. The other piece of attire they all had was the B-suit, a bulletproof shield that covered the chest, back and groin areas while maintaining good mobility. The heat didn't help, but it was the safe thing to do.

His major worry was the damn drones. They were constantly overhead, ever since they became popular in the 10's. Their camera resolution allowed the observer to check how that pimple on your cheek was changing from day-to-day. If they wanted to, they could even refer to their scanned database for the pimple's changing shape or color as the days went by.

They had a solution for that problem, but it wasn't foolproof. This was going to be a masquerade party/rally. Everyone came in some kind of facial disguise. But there were times when you had to take the mask off to drink, to eat and in this heat to wipe your brow.

It was time to begin. He made sure the speaker was turned on and he gave a test cough into his mike. He heard the cough clearly in his ear buds. "OK, people, we're going to get started here, so please listen up and we'll cover some ground rules. We won't want to upset any Peacers today. Let's let them provoke any nastiness if they want to."

He rattled off the rules they had decided on in the previous weeks as they prepared for this event. No violence toward anyone. No littering. No alcohol or drugs at this gathering.

"I don't think anyone here is stupid enough to be packing, but if you are, keep it out of sight." He wasn't afraid for the Peacers to hear this last item because he was sure they knew that people were packing guns.

"OK, so, how many of you remember The Constitution of the United States?" he asked. There was a general reaction that could be taken as a collective chuckle. "I mean it though, how many of you had ever read a copy of it?"

About 80% of the crowd raised their hand. "Cool, so you all know that our Founding Fathers had this idea that people should be in charge of the government; the government was supposed to only do the things that individual couldn't practically do for themselves, not even in organized private groups. So what were the primary purposes of the federal government?"

A guy in a clown mask hollered out, "To protect the country from foreigners, uh… like defense."

"To regulate commerce between the various states," shouted a girl with a cat's hood over her head.

A guy with a black hood covering his whole head and just two small holes for the eyes called out: "To make laws that are required to protect the rights of individuals so that they don't wind up screwing each other by taking other people's properties, beating the shit out of them and so on."

This went on for a bit and nobody mentioned things like take care of the poor, provide subsidies to businesses and farmers, care for the sick and all the other stuff the feds are doing now.

As he was listening and scanning the crowd, he noticed that the Peacers were positioning themselves around the perimeter of the crowd. His trained eye could spot the carefully hidden riot gear; they looked like ordinary citizens, in sweats, jeans, polo shirts and baseball caps. Yet under their outer layers Hugo could see the kevtite garment. Kevtite was an ultra strong material made of Kevlar and titanium. It was nearly impenetrable by anything but armor piercing. Of course a slug from an 87 would punch a guy pretty good and possibly knock him down. The other tell-tale sign was the utility bag they carried that contained their headgear. They didn't want to stand out like sore thumbs, so they kept their headgear off until needed.

Hugo didn't like the looks of it in any case. There were so many of them. He noticed one guy in the regular Peacer uniform slowly making his way to where he and Saul were standing. He had his eyes fixed on Hugo.

When the Peacer reached Hugo, he asked: "Can I see your permit please?"

Hugo said: "Don't need a permit."

"I'm sure you are familiar with City Ordinance #20347689, all gatherings in public and private places require a permit."

"Maybe, but I'm sure you are aware that that ordinance is superseded by the Constitution of the United States, Amendment I, which, as of now, hasn't been repealed. Just in case you don't recall it, 'Congress shall make no law respecting ... the right of the people to peaceably assemble'. There are no qualifications or restrictions mentioned. So, you are out of line even asking for a permit."

"Regular wise guy, eh?" the Peacer said as he reached for Hugo's Batman mask.

Hugo moved backwards to escape his reach and he said: "You touch me without a warrant, you're going to suffer the consequences. I am here on a peaceful mission and not causing any trouble. Don't you be the one to start the trouble."

The Peacer, who was taller than average, nodded his head vigorously and all of a sudden three more Peacers materialized out of the crowd. They all had rather large masks in the shape of animal heads; there was a tiger a lion and a jaguar. When they saw the Peacer in uniform nod his head, they took off their masks and revealed the riot headgear they had on underneath.

"You are under arrest for obstructing justice," the lead Peacer said.

Hugo was not going to jail. That was simply not an option. Nobody was sure, but once they had you in their clutches nothing good was going to happen. People simply didn't know because people didn't come back to talk about it. He pulled his Colt and shouted: "Stop! I am defending myself against open aggression started by you. One more step and I'll take you out."

The Peacers stopped in their tracks. It seemed that they didn't want to turn this into a riot. The cordon of Peacers at the periphery all at once donned their riot headgear and took out their lunners, laser stunners.

The head Peacer pointed at Hugo with an outstretched arm. Moments later, Hugo saw a weird ray of light surround him. It seemed to come from above, right through the canopy of the tree above him. As soon as he figured out that it came from above, he felt a blow to his gut that caused him to double over. He fell to the ground, doubled up in agony. He tried to figure out what happened. Despite the pain in his gut, he was fully conscious and his mind put the pieces together.

The Peacer's outstretched arm was a signal to the drone operator who unleashed a beam that was targeted right at Hugo's gut. *Damn, he thought, that's new. Didn't see that coming, not even any hints in the news or his regular underground sources of the latest feds development programs. That was a surgical strike.*

As he was carried out of the crowd, he had just a second to meet Saul's eyes and he saw him shrug, as if to say sorry pal. That took a moment to sink in. Tears welled up in his eyes as it dawned on him that Saul had sold him out.

=====================

We hold these truths to be self-evident:
That all men are created equal,
That they are endowed by their Creator with certain unalieable rights, including Life, Liberty and the pursuit of Happiness.

That to secure these rights, governments are instituted among men, deriving their just powers from the consent of the governed.

That whenever any form of government becomes destructive to these ends, it is the right of the people to alter or to abolish it, and to institute new government, laying its foundation on such principles and organizing its powers in such form, as to them shall seem most likely to effect their safety and happiness.

Prudence, indeed, will dictate that governments long established should not be changed for light and transient causes; and accordingly all experience hath shown that mankind are more disposed to suffer, while evils are sufferable, than to right themselves by abolishing the forms to which they are accustomed. But when a long train of abuses and usurpations, pursuing invariably the same object evinces a design to reduce them under absolute despotism, it is their right, it is their duty, to throw off such government, and to provide new guards for their future security.

This is the text of the Declaration of Independence by the colonists of America in 1776, modified slightly but immaterially, for readability. It is an amazing, daring and blatant statement by a people very far removed from their seat of government, ill supplied for any military action and hardly unified in their local governments and affairs. Each colony had its own industry or agriculture and its own perspective on how to manage their populations in civil and criminal matters. Yet the one thing they had in common was the hatred they had for the British government. That hatred created such a strong force of unity that these colonists were willing to put all they had, life, liberty and honor on the line. We all know what the outcome of that improbable conflict was.

This Declaration has no legal bearing today. It was merely a statement to the British government that we had had enough and weren't going to play their game any more. In stead, a few years later, the colonists created "that other earth shattering" document, the Constitution of the United States of America. Yet the Declaration is of utmost importance today as it set the foundation for the Constitution, for the way these colonies wished to be governed and to secure the rights enumerated in the Declaration. Similarly, today the Declaration holds the key to understanding the purpose and the legitimacy of the Constitution.

The Constitution, along with the first set of Amendments, the so-called Bill of Rights, establishes what powers the federal government should have and which rights of the people may not be violated. It is called the "supreme law" of the land and it states that no laws in conflict with it shall be passed. In light of the American Revolution, and the issues spelled out in the Declaration, the Founding Fathers insisted on a limited government, structured into the three branches of legislature, executive and judiciary, which would take care of the central, federal issues that individual states could not practically or effectively handle. These were primarily the following:

> To provide for national defense against foreign enemies
> To regulate international commerce
> To enter and adhere to international treaties
> To coin a national currency, collect taxes, duties, imposts and excises for the common defense and general welfare of the United States
> To establish post offices and roads
> To promote progress of science and useful arts by granting copyrights
> To punish pirates and perpetrators of felonies committed on the high seas
> To declare war and make rules regarding prisoners of war
> To provide for an army and a navy (later by extension of the technology an air force)
> To call forth the militia to suppress uprisings and invasions
> To establish and govern a seat of government, and
> To make all laws necessary for carrying into execution of these powers.

Following these express, limited powers of the federal government, the Founding Fathers sought to establish a bill of rights for the protection of specific individual rights. These were expressed in the first ten amendments to the Constitution and ratified in 1791. Chief among those rights were:

> Freedom of religion
> Freedom of speech
> Right to assemble and petition the government for grievances
> Right to keep and bear arms
> Protection against unreasonable searches

Protection against searches without specific warrants

Right to trial by a jury for capital and other infamous crimes

Protection from testifying against himself

Just compensation for property taken for public use

Due process of law for deprivation of life, liberty or property

Right to a speedy and public trial

Right to confrontation with witnesses against him

Protection from excessive bail and fines

Protection against cruel and unusual punishment.

This overview of the Constitution gives you the core thinking and purpose of our Founding Fathers as they created this new nation. We Americans have enjoyed the fruits of this labor over the intervening years. And this political system, which was the ultimate design of a representative democracy, has been "exported" to many other countries since.

Unfortunately, the Constitution of the United States of America is dying. Actually it is lingering a long death. The malady started shortly after its adoption. But it was a slow progression of a disease until the early part of the 20th Century, when it suffered a major assault from what has become known as the Progressive Movement. The term Progressive is in itself ironic, as it represents, in this country, anything but progress. Rather, with regards to the Constitution and the liberties of the American people, it has represented a terribly regressive effect on our society.

Some people would argue that what the government has done in the last 100 years or so, is good. I mean we have free education; we have Social Security and Medicare; we have unemployment insurance and subsidies to farmers and businesses; and all manner of handouts from the government. How can that be bad? I don't need to tell you, dear reader, that it is becoming increasingly obvious that the government doles are being paid for by others. The government has become a great funnel for our tax dollars and the rulers of this country determine how to distribute that money. In other words, what to do with the fruits of our labors.

When you consider what our Founding Fathers envisioned and compare that with what we have today, you will quickly realize that it is completely different. Alas, our Founding Fathers were aware of the pitfalls and tried their best to stave off this collapse into bureaucratic tyranny. George Washington once sated that: "The power under the Constitution will always be with the people." He could not have foreseen the persistency and the salesmanship of the Progressives.

As early as 1823, Thomas Jefferson remarked: "Let us carry ourselves back to the time when the Constitution was adopted [all of 46 years at that time], recollect the spirit manifest in the debates and instead of trying what meaning may be squeezed out of the text, or invented against it, conform to the probable one in which it was passed." As early as that, the Constitution was under attack. Politicians and judges started to apply meanings and interpretations to the text that were contrary to the spirit of the documents.

How can you tell? Where is this spirit of the Constitution? It is to be found in the well documented debates of 1778 known as the Federalist Papers and the Antifederalist Papers. Therein you will find the true intent of the Founding Fathers. There you will find the fears of what might become. It was so well expressed by James Madison, who said: "If men were angels, no government would be necessary; if angels were to govern, no external and internal controls on government would be necessary."

The Antifederalists expressed the greatest concern over a "strong" federal government. They feared that a federal government, imbued with powers over the States and the American citizens was something to be feared. They realized that power tends to corrupt and they saw no reason it would not do so in this country. The war of independence had thrown off the shackle of a ruthless government in the form of King George III of England. They were intent on preventing a resurgence of such a state of affairs.

We Americans have been somewhat lulled into complacency since, I suppose, we do not have a monarch to worry about. We are quite comfortable with relying on our representatives to take care of things, even though they too are not angels.

While there had been pressure on the Constitution and its meaning since its adoption, the real jolt came in 1912, when President Woodrow Wilson declared: "All that progressives ask or desire I permission...to interpret the Constitution according to the Darwinian principle... Some citizens of this country have never got beyond the Declaration of Independence, signed in Philadelphia, July 4th, 1776... the Declaration of Independence did not mention the questions of our day." In other words, he said that old document is no longer relevant because things have changed.

To this author it is a fearsome challenge to visualize what concepts of the Declaration of Independence are no longer relevant. Is it that all men are NOT created equal? If so, how are the distinctions made? Which of us is so unequal as to have fewer rights than others? Which of us is destined to rule over others and by what determining characteristic?

Or is it that when a government becomes destructive to the rights of life, liberty and the pursuit of happiness of any men that people no longer have a right to "alter or abolish it?" I'm scratching my head here, but it seems the Progressives do indeed believe a government once installed is there to stay, no matter how corrupt or repressive it becomes. When you say the Declaration is no longer applicable, this is what you are saying.

Or is the Declaration no longer relevant because the following practices should now be acceptable:

Cutting off trade

Imposing taxes without the people's consent

Depriving people of the right to trial by jury

Abolishing local laws

Creating a multitude of offices and departments to harass the people and collect their substance

Forbidding local government to pass laws of immediate and pressing importance

Refusing to pass laws of accommodation for the people lest they give up their right of representation

Dissolving the House of Representatives repeatedly

Blocking the administration of justice by refusing to allow the judiciary to function

Making judges dependent on the executive branch of government

Rendering the armed forces superior to Civil power

From the list above, we can readily recognize recurrences of those unacceptable conditions. The multitude of government agencies and departments of this and that (the fourth branch) control our lives, businesses, freedom and pursuits of happiness. The armed forces in this country have all the military power; the people are helpless. Fees are imposed without due process or consent.

These were the chief grievances enumerated in the Declaration and that sparked the uprising of the colonists to create a new nation. It is troubling to me that any lover of freedom and liberty could consider these practices to again be acceptable. Declaring that the Declaration is no longer relevant is making exactly that claim. Of course, if you are in a role of governmental leadership, or any governmental function for that matter, you might well subscribe to abolishing the principles of the Declaration. After all, they are an obstacle to your power grab. But that is exactly what the Founding Fathers wanted to do to prevent a recurrence of an oppressive government.

From the time of Wilson's declaration in 1912, things

have gotten worse. The so-called Progressive movement turned into the liberal movement and lately has resumed the title of Progressives. The resulting changes to the relationship between the American people and its government have created a society that is ever more embracing the ideal of socialism, that is, we want equal handouts, regardless of what we have put in. The very size of the federal government is a sure indicator of the spread of federal powers far beyond what the Founding Fathers envisioned.

Surveys Rassmussen Reports in late 2011 indicate that a mere 17-20% of likely voters in this country believe that the U.S. Government has the consent of the Governed. Wow, is that a government run amuck or what? Add to that situations of the federal government suing the States for enforcing the federal law, harassing and discouraging businesses and the entrepreneurial spirit that made this country great with endless regulations and prohibitions, harassing law-abiding citizens when they try to defend themselves or their property, and dumping a mountain of debt on future generations, and you have a serious mix of a brew for a new revolution in this country to shake off the shackles once more.

As if that was not enough, there are signs of things getting much worse. In my opinion, what we are doing is supporting those who would see us all giving up our freedom and hand it over to the government; exactly one of the great fears of our Founding Fathers. It is also a sure way to provide an open road for some despot to gain control of our government and do away with the great form of government originally envisioned by our Founding Fathers. I can just see your raised eyebrows as you read this, dear reader, but the people of Germany in the 1930s would never have supported Hitler if they had any idea of where he was heading. By the time he made his plans clear, it was too late; he had solid control of the military and police.

Any student of popular literature, I suspect, has read George Orwell's "1984". If you have not, dear reader, you owe it to yourself to read that book. I mean it, it's a mandate. Failure to do so is a definite decision on your part to surrender your freedoms and to trust the government with your life, your belongings, you ability to conduct the business of your dreams, your savings and your old age security. If you do not believe me, read on; I will demonstrate.

In *1984* Orwell paints a picture of a despotic government that is so suppressive, it is hard for us American citizens to imagine it as anything but a fictitious fantasy. In that book, the arch villain is "Big Brother" who represents the government. That government has total control over its citizens' actions, behavior and thoughts. All people are under constant scrutiny via cameras and microphones; there is NO privacy, not even in the people's homes, including the bedroom. The language is controlled so that "impure thoughts" are not even possible. The concept of free thought and dreams has been eradicated. The ultimate goal of the government is to make crime all but impossible because the would-be criminal would be detected and intercepted long before he or she could carry out their act.

While this is perhaps a bit extreme and still hard to visualize as reality in America, let us consider how far we have come.

1. In the twentieth century, more than 60,000 women underwent forced sterilization under the pretext of eliminating undesirables. In the U.S., 32 states had eugenics laws targeted at minorities and the poor.

2. Federal officials are using a loophole in a 1986 law that allows warrant less searches of stored communications.

3. Google has engaged in "Project Glass" which is a wearable computer with built-in camera. This allows the wearer to record in video and audio

format everything that goes on before them. The potential for invading others' privacy is unlimited.

4.   Drones are being deployed in civilian situations, currently under the guise of apprehending and observing criminals. The city of Lancaster, California, insists that it will use the drones only to fight crime. Local law enforcement officials are thrilled about the system as it will help to spot home invasion robberies, track unsuspecting criminals, and locate car accidents to assist patrol response, for example. Supposedly great care is being exercised to ensure that the operation of the drones would observe privacy issues via a code of conduct. The advocates of this technology are bending over backwards to try to assure the American public that this will not unduly invade their privacy. Hah! That's how things start. An initial inroad is made with very limited application to assuage the wary. But, once the technology is in place, its use can only go up. In a few years, a decade maybe, we will be so used to the unmanned planes in the sky above us that we will hardly notice the increased use that they are bound to be put to.

5.   Companies that you do business with are allowed, by default, to disclose your information to others. You have the right to block this disclosure, but only by taking action. I doubt that many of us make the effort to do that. What this means is that as a matter of course, your privacy is invaded and broadcast to people over which you have no control. Currently this seems to be a relatively small thing, but the potential misuse is huge. It is another form of the ability for others to spy on your activities.

6.   The internet is infamous for its proliferation of private information of its users. When you go on the internet, you are for all intents and purposes naked, figuratively. The ability of "Big Brother" to observe your behavior is well established. Thank God that this doesn't seem to be abused too badly for now, but the potential is unlimited.

7.   Companies with "800-type" phone numbers now have an automatic number identification system in place. This allows them to capture the caller's phone number, name and address. This data is fed into huge databases and you can imagine the potential for abuse in this area.

8.   For some reason, the City of San Francisco intends to place a proposal to ban circumcisions on the ballot. It's not clear to me what the reasoning is for such a law, other than perhaps to stop "physical abuse" of babies and minors. While I have my own philosophy about this matter, this seems to be clearly a matter of the government deciding what the right behavior for its citizens is, even overriding their religious customs and rights.

9.   The recording industry is pushing for a law that allows searches of CD and DVD makers' premises without a search warrant. Apparently the piracy has gotten out of hand and some business interests think that violating a basic right guaranteed by the Constitution of the United States is justified "in this instance." Perhaps, but then we open the door to allowing warrant-less searches for other reasons and before you realize what happened, the need for warrants is gone entirely.

10.   The so-called "Obamacare" health bill is another example of "Big Brother" deciding what you must do.   Unlike a car for which you must carry insurance in order to drive it, which is still a choice you can make, health insurance is now something that you must buy because you don't have a choice to live or die. Since you go on living, you are now required to buy insurance for yourself, rather than risking the extra costs of medical services when you have no insurance.

11.   The right to eminent domain is being abused by forcing private citizens to sell their property so that a private company, such as a developer, can get their way without proper compensation to the individual. Granted, it may make sense to remove the old structure so that there will be room for the new, but that property can be bought at some price. You know the old saying: "Everything has its price."   Maybe that individual property owner wants a totally unreasonable price, like $100 million for a half acre plot. Unfortunately our illustrious Supreme Court ruled that private property can be taken to make way for private development, in direct violation of the Constitution of the United States. I guess oaths of office no longer have any meaning either; the judges swear an oath to support and defend the Constitution. But, "Big Brother" knows best.

12.   Some police agencies want to use GPS devices mounted clandestinely on suspects' cars. In this case, the Supreme Court ruled that the clandestine installation of GPS tracking devices on suspects' vehicles by police without a warrant violates the right of an individual to be free from unreasonable

searches. For now, "Big Brother" has not yet won this one. Keep an eye on that in the future.

13. One of the central themes in Orwell's *1984* is "doublethink". This refers to the use of language to impart meanings to words that are opposite to the actual terminology. It was the government's way of controlling and revising reality to suit its current purpose. "Doublethink" meant the power to hold two contradictory beliefs in one's mind simultaneously. Today, as of this writing, we have a stark example of this exact concept going on.

With the notorious health insurance mandate bill, which requires all Americans to obtain health insurance, we now have the government telling the governed how they shall behave and what they shall buy. Apparently, if an individual is discovered to not be carrying health insurance, he or she will be taxed or penalized a certain amount of money. But, in order for our illustrious Supreme Court justices to rule on the legality of that bill, they had to engage in "doublethink". Specifically, in order for the Supreme Court to consider the legality of that bill, the mandatory health insurance "incentive" had to be called a penalty, rather than a tax (the Supreme Court can't rule on tax matters). But to support the legality of the bill the Court had to call it a tax so that Congress would have the power to impose it as a tax.

Furthermore, the justices decided that Congress did not have the power to regulate doing nothing but it did have the power to tax people for doing nothing. In this case the "nothing" is not buying health insurance. Apparently in our Supreme Court's doublethink mode regulating does not include taxing. In other words, taxing is not considered an act of regulating individuals' behavior.

14. The Occupy movements, that started with "Occupy Wall Street" and have moved across the country, have given rise to numerous violations of Constitutional rights. "Big Brother" surely has been active in this arena. Protesters are routinely arrested at the site of their protests. The Constitution gives the right to peacefully assemble to all citizens. It does not provide any special conditions, nor exclusions to that right. Yet, as municipalities and other government units grow weary of the protesters, they decide to find some excuse to stop the assembly of Americans. Local governments now routinely require a permit for assembling. A permit implies the possibility of denying the permit and thus you have a restriction on assembly.

15. As discussed under "Guns", the issue of mental illness (or more bluntly put: insanity) presents a challenge for our society. According to various studies of the link between mental illness and violence, there appears to be such a link. Yet even with that link, the percentage of mentally ill people who commit violent crimes is about the same as the percentage of "healthy" people. "Big Brother's" approach would be to incarcerate those who are diagnosed as mentally ill and try to "fix" them.

In our present day, we are trying to decide whether to do that as well. There appears to be some pressure to identify people with mental illness, as well as those who have undergone some stress, such as rejection by a loved one, loss of a job, divorce, for example. Studies are under way to track the behavior of mass murderers to see if there is some predictable pattern. The idea is to see if we can intercept the crime before it is carried out. Does this remind anyone of the movie "The Minority Report"? So far, very few predictors, such as criminal history, a sense of victimization, a certain age range, have been identified but not with any definitive certainty.

The struggle between the people and their government is as old as government itself. Our Founding Fathers tried so very hard to assure that the power over people shall reside with the people, not the government. In other words, the government shall serve the people, not the other way around. The Founding Fathers were divided over how much power to give to the federal government. In framing the Constitution, they stipulated that the powers of the federal government are specifically enumerated in the Constitution, and all remaining powers are left with the States and individuals. But, since angels are not in government, those in positions of power continue to broaden their power; it's a natural trait of human beings. Consequently, "Big Brother" continues to gain ground.

Apart from the examples listed above, our government, Federal and State, have declared power for themselves far beyond what the Founding Fathers envisioned and intended. Our government has become a bureaucratic administrator of finance, trade, research and development, education, social welfare, farm production, just to name a few. One must presume that the people, through their representatives, have chosen that this should be so. And I personally benefit from this system by collecting Social Security and having Medicare health coverage. I, as all the rest of us, really had no choice once the systems were put in place. We were (are) forced to pay into the Social Security system and Medicare. Consequently, we want our "investment" back.

Just as George Orwell depicted advanced technology for his era, as a basis for enabling Big Brother's power, so do we face application of technology for better or wore. The ever advancing technology is probably the main threat to individual rights. The technology allows tracking and control of individuals' behavior to an extent not imaginable just 10 years ago. Needless to say, this will continue. To what use this technology is put, remains to be seen. Just be aware that "Big Brother" is in there and rubbing his hands. We have put ourselves into the hands of "Big Brother."

Each of the examples presented above may be considered small issues of no great importance by themselves. As a result, we are lulled into complacency as just one more, tiny inch of relative little importance is gained by the government. Well, just as the glaciers in Alaska seem to be standing still, they ultimately reach their destination. Similarly, ultimately, "Big Brother" will gain full control and then it will be too late.

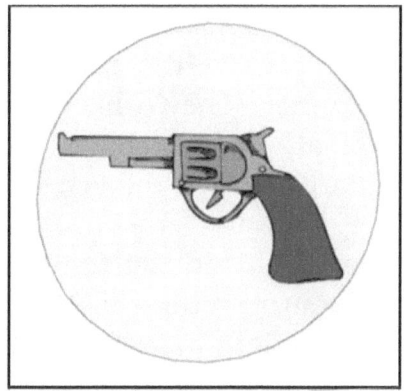

Crime Prevention & Guns

He loved making the climb up to the ridge. The view was worth it every time. Under the practically clear, deep blue Idaho sky he saw the lake between the pine trees. An occasional meadow peaked through the gaps in the trees, adding that bright green color to the dark green of the pines. A puffy white cloud was hanging just over the center of the gap in the trees, above the lake, and he saw its reflection in the mirror smooth surface of the lake. Despite the gentle breeze that wafted over his face, bringing that special outdoors aroma of fresh air, so sweet that he became aware of his nostrils, the lake remained absolutely placid.

But he was noticing that it got harder to make this climb every time. His knees just weren't what they used to be. As he sat on the rock with his feet dangling over the edge, his eyes took in all that he owned. The mirror surface of the lake adjacent to his land reflected the deep blue Idaho sky with just that one cloud in sight. The pine trees covered every acre of land; land that had been in his family for ten generations. It covered just about one hundred acres.

Bart never got married himself though and he had to

wonder what would happen to this land when he died. He was trying to figure out who the best beneficiary might be. He had cousins, but they just didn't have the sense of appreciation for this unspoiled wilderness. They'd likely try to commercialize it. Good luck with that. The feds have been trying to pry this land away from Bart now for the last five years.

He was sure of one thing: he would not let the feds have it. They wanted to annex it to the surrounding Sawtooth National Forest. But Bart was willing to fight to the death to keep the feds from taking this land away from his family.

There was one lad in the family that he liked, his grand-nephew Danny. Danny was the grandson of his young sister Ellie and her husband Luke. He had an energy about him and a curiosity about all kinds of things that went beyond his 15 years of age. One look at Danny, and you could tell that he was special. He had that aura of confidence and knowing what to do and he wasn't afraid of anything.

Danny came to visit last year and spent his Summer vacation on Bart's ranch. The two of them became like a couple of boys having the adventure of their lives. Hunting, fishing, swimming in Blue Pool, mountain climbing and spending time in Bart's airplane soaring over the mountains.

One afternoon, as they hiked up Spine Hill, they came to a clearing in the trees and saw a black bear rummaging for berries. Bart held out his hand to stop Danny and motioned for him to be quiet. He must have raised his hand too suddenly because Danny bumped into it hard and suffered a sudden coughing spell.

The bear heard that and was suddenly on full alert, up on his hind quarters and scanning the surrounding area.

"Shhhhh!" Bart whispered, trying to get Danny to stop his coughing. But it was too late. The bear caught sight of them and started to lumber up the hill towards them.

It was time to find refuge. If that bear felt they were in his territory, they were in a heap of trouble. Bart knew of a cave just a few hundred feet up the hill. It had a wide entrance but narrowed down to a point where one man could squeeze through the opening into the large cavern beyond. If they could reach that, they could wait out the bear, he would eventually give up when he realized he couldn't reach his prey.

"That way and run, we have enough of a lead on that bear that we can reach the cave before him," Bart said to Danny, not at all as confident as he tried to sound. They grabbed their gear and hightailed it up the mountain. Bart hoped the bear would lose sight of them long enough for him to stop and try to pick up their trail. The bear hadn't reached the spot where he first saw the hikers, so he hadn't picked up their scent yet.

The terrain was a combination of rock and lose gravel, making progress slower than Bart liked. Neither of them had taken the time to strap their backpacks back onto the back and carrying it by the top strap was awkward at a moment like this. But he didn't dare stop to put them on properly. Bart could see Danny struggling with his as well.

"Just drop it if it's too much. We'll hope the bear won't find it and go after the food. The food is wrapped anyway, so it might be alright," Bart huffed the words out between steps.

"I'm ok, Uncle Bart," he replied. Bart could see the strain of the load on the lad's face though, but he didn't want to force the issue. His pride was at stake.

The cave was just another 100 feet ahead of them and Bart thought they might make it OK. That's when he heard the roar of the bear, right on their heels, not more than 75 feet away.

"Move it, Danny, don't stop don't look around and drop that pack. Get into that cave and then crawl through the opening at the far end. I'll be right behind you."

As he followed on Danny's heels, he was trying to decide whether to make a stand with his gun and take the bear down. He didn't want to do that though. This was his territory too and Bart always felt that the black bear in particular was a majestic animal. But it may come down to a matter of life and death. If that were the case, Bart was determined to win. He crossed a patch of loose gravel, about 30 feet from the cave. Bart dropped his pack and scooped up a fistful of gravel, turned and stood up to face that bear. He flung the gravel full force at the bear who was within 20 feet of him now. That surprised the bear and he came to a stop with a look of confusion upon him. Bart scooped up another handful and flung it at the bear. The bear let out a roar that was about to shatter Bart's ear drum. He took a quick look over his shoulder to see how Danny was making out and saw that he was just inside the mouth of the cave.

Bart picked up his pack and started to sprint after Danny. He was really huffing now and thought his lungs were about to burst. His knees were killing him. As he entered the cave, he saw Danny's feet disappearing through the hole at the other end. Bart ran for the hole and threw his pack, walking stick, rifle and canteen through the hole and got on his knees to crawl through. He could see that the bear had reached the cave. The light against the far end of the cave dimmed from the blocked sunlight as the bear filled much of the cave entrance with his body.

Bart was half way through the hole when he felt the bear's paw on his left leg. He grit his teeth as the claws dug into his leg and felt the pull of the bear. He was trying to pull Bart back out of the hole. Bart gave a turn of his whole body to try to lose the grip of the claw and it worked. He pulled his leg away and scrambled further through the hole. The bear was really ticked off that the pray had escaped him, but he started to try to dig his way into the hole. Thank God that it was hard rock and the bear didn't make any progress.

Safe on the other side, Bart looked around and noticed that nothing had changed since the last time he had visited here. It was still dark in the inner cave as the bear continued to try to get through the hole, blocking most of the bit of light that normally made its way into the second cavern. Bart wanted to survey the damage to his leg. It hurt like hell and he could feel the blood oozing out of the wounds. By then, Danny had dug out his flashlight and the two of them looked at the mauled leg.

Bart had a spare towel in his pack and he got that out to form a bandage around his lower leg.

"Wait a minute, Uncle Bart, let me clean that up first. Don't want that getting infected." Danny rummaged in his pack, which he decided to hang on to rather than drop it, and found the first aid kit. There wasn't much hydrogen peroxide in the small bottle, but it had to do. He poured it over the wound, trying to spread it over the deep holes. Next, he took the towel and tore it in two, down lengthwise. He soaked one part of it in water from his canteen and gently washed away the blood and peroxide. The wounds were deep and fresh blood kept oozing out. Danny then took the other half of the towel and wrapped it tightly around the leg.

"Does it hurt, Uncle Bar?" Danny asked, and immediately thought what a dumb question that was. Of course it must hurt. Quite a bit of flesh was torn away. "Sorry, dumb question, you don't have to answer that."

"Well, Danny, I must say I've felt better and I've felt worse. I'll be OK." But the reality was that he felt the wound throb with pain and he had to exert great effort not to let it show in his face.

"I think we'll just rest here for a while," Bart said. He needed to catch his breath. The anxiety of the attack had all but stopped his heart and breathing. And, even with the tending to the wounds, his heart was still racing.

The bear was still growling and trying to claw his way through the hole, but with less enthusiasm. They just kept an eye on him, hoping he wouldn't find a crack in the rock and wind up enlarging that hole. That would not be good.

It was getting darker as the sun set and they knew they'd have to spend the night here. There was no way they would risk hiking back home in the dark. Especially not with a pissed off bear around.

They made themselves as comfortable as possible. Danny took charge of making the sleeping arrangements. It was still middle of Summer and the temperature would be tolerable. For dinner they munched some of the energy bars they had brought, saving the trail mix for later. Their water supply was not large but for now it was not a point of worry. They settled down and sleep found them both, despite the excitement of the afternoon.

Bart woke sometime after sunrise, judging by the light coming through the hole. He turned around to see how Danny was doing and saw that he was not in his sleeping bag. With a start of panic, Bart tried to get up but immediately realized that the pain in his leg was excruciating. Even so, he tried to stand up and pulled himself up by a ledge in the rock wall. When he tried to put weight on his left leg, he almost cried out. *Wow, that's not fun. I won't be running on this leg for a while.* Just then, Danny came crawling through the hole. He pushed his gun and a couple of canteens ahead of him.

"Oh, hi, Uncle Bart. How are you doing this morning?"

"I'm OK, but where the hell did you go off to? You scared the living shit out of me."

"Just went to get some water and look for berries. Found some too." he said with a big wide grin on his face. From his pocket he emptied a plastic bag full of blackberries.

"Damn, don't you know that bear could still be lingering around?"

"Yeah, but I took a good look and I had the gun loaded and ready to shoot if he decided to come back at me. Didn't see hide or hair of him though.

"Thought I might find some firewood next, to make breakfast. You're gonna need your strength today, Uncle. We can make a fire pit just outside that narrow hole, in the outer cave, to keep the smoke outa here."

Yes, that was quite an adventure last Summer. Turned

out Bart couldn't move on his own power. Danny went down the mountain into town to get help. One tough kid, he is, knew just what to do and wasn't afraid of what he might find on the way back, all by himself. He returned late that next day with some forest rangers and a rescue cot to carry him down the mountain.

Bart could see Danny taking over this place and keeping it in the family. That would please him a mighty lot. He decided to invite him back this year to talk about it. He'd be 16 about then and Bart had confidence that Danny could make a decision about it.

Later that Summer, Danny came for that visit. Bart explained his thoughts about the property and what he'd like to see happen to it. Danny asked Bart to think it over a few days. While they hunted, fished and flew over the landscape, not a word was said on the subject. On the last night of his visit, Danny explained to Bart, that he would be proud to carry on the protection of this property by the family. He explained that he gave it serious thought, considering the responsibility as well as the opportunity that came along with owning this land. Bart was convinced that he had made the right choice. Any other kid of that age might have simply said "yes" the moment the offer was made. But Danny had enough maturity and common sense to see that it was not a simple choice. He realized that there came a significant responsibility with this land.

"I'll make arrangements in my will to transfer this land into your hands upon my death," he explained and they drank a toast.

"Don't tell your parents I served you alcohol or they'll have my hide," he said with a grin.

"No worries, this isn't my first alcohol," Danny said grinning in response.

The challenge for Bart now was how to stave off the Feds. They were getting more and more insistent in their demand for him to vacate the land.

The following morning, he drove into town to pick up things he needed and to get his mail. There was a letter from the Department of Agriculture. Bart's heart began to beat faster, as it always did when he received a letter from the DoA, which managed the Forest Service. He opened the envelope when he got back into his truck. He read: "Dear Mr. Bowing, this letter is to inform you that the Department of Agriculture has ruled that the property known as the Bowing Ranch, and described in the reference above, will be annexed into the Sawtooth National Forest effective three months from the date of this letter. You have until that time to vacate the property and remove only your personal effects. This decision has a long history of process and procedure, as you are aware." There was more to the letter, but that was the gist of it.

So, this is it. They intend to take it by force, Bart thought as he drove home. *Well, Danny, I'm sorry it came to this. I don't know if I can hold them off.*

It was time to get serious about making plans on how he would handle the Feds' assault. He had already made up his mind that they were not going to get it without a fight.

He decided to take care of his will the next day, to make sure that the land would go to Danny, in case he prevailed.

The next several weeks were spent in mobilizing his defenses. The property was well suited for defense; it had only one easy access route through the canyon. That was the road, a simple, narrow single lane asphalt strip with occasional turnouts to accommodate passing vehicles, should they ever meet on that road. The rest of the property was reachable only over rocky hills. Vehicles were not going to work there, not even off-roads. If they intended to approach him other than by the road, they would have to scramble over those rocks and through the pine forest.

He had established several defensive positions to cover his whole terrain and a series of dirt roads connected them into a network that allowed him to move quickly to any point as the need arose. It had to be effective as this was a one-man show. He could not involve any of his friends in the active defense of his property.

He had installed surveillance cameras and sensors to alert him of any unexpected visitors. It was normally shut off; else he'd be jumping for every deer or bear that wondered onto his property. Bart tested it on Monday and it all worked just fine except one sensor got blocked with bird shit of all things. That must have been a freak shot; normally that wouldn't affect the sensors with their sun visor shields.

As to his arsenal, it was one of his pride and joys. All purchased on the black market and he had no idea how they got hold of the stuff. Even the ordnance was from the black market. He had enough stuff to lay waste to a battalion if need be.

The heavy duty gun was his pair of M-240Bs. One was mounted on the roof of his Hummer and he could operate it by standing in the specially fitted moon roof. Its 7.62mm ammo provided enough punch for anything he figured he'd encounter in the terrain of his ranch. That Hummer never left the ranch, it wasn't exactly something he wanted to show off. The other was intended for deployment into terrain where he couldn't drive that Hummer, which was little enough.

For high mobility and quick deployment he had his choice of an M40A1 sniper rifle, a M25 sniper rifle and his M16A2. He had his fourth generation Glock as a personal side arm. The new dual recoil spring made shooting this gun almost as smooth as butter in comparison to the previous versions.

The Feds had mounted a stiff legal assault on his property over the last five years. They had offered a paltry $200,000, $2000 per acre. It was laughable but their argument was that it was not suited for commercial purposes and was "just idle land in the middle of a national forest." He had countered at $2 million, knowing that that was overpriced, but that was his prerogative. The negotiations had fallen down about nine months ago and so here he was.

Their justification for eminent domain was that the ranch was surrounded by the national forest and that it should be converted to public property to make the land contiguous. He had easements to retain access to his ranch across the national forest property and his counter argument was that the land had never been part of the national forest, for whatever reasons and taking it now would be no different that extending the outer boundaries of the forest land. The ranch was not in a "strategic" location for Forest Service purposes, such as the need to enlarge a camp ground or to build an access road, or anything else. It was simply a land grabbing scheme.

On the day after the deadline stated in their last letter, he was up early and a bit tense, picturing how they might arrive and try to take over the land. He had positioned his Hummer in an elevated canyon that had a good view of the approach road. He had made sure that his generator was well stocked with fuel and that all his systems were up. He had coverage of much of his ranch with the wireless towers that were positioned on the hill tops. The Hummer had a monitoring station in it to show the approaches to his ranch.

At about 9:00 am the signal went off, "Beep, beep, beep, beep," it went and Bart jumped to alertness, scanning his screens and the sensor panel. *So, they decided to simply come up his road, just like a milk man on a delivery,* Bart thought, smiling to himself. There were three of them. He saw Ben, the forest ranger, in their midst. Ben had been in the group that rescued Bart from the cave after that bear attack. That figured, he was probably the most familiar with the ranch. He'd visited often enough. Bart and he were friends, but things had gotten a bit strained during the last two years, as the negotiations got more testy. Ben had nothing to do with the negotiations, of course, but it was his agency that Bart had to deal with.

He jumped into his buggy and drove down the road to

meet them. When he was about 100 feet away from them, he turned the buggy sideways to block most of the road, even though the buggy wasn't long enough to block it totally.

"Mornin' Ben," he shouted, "what brings you and your friends here today?"

"Awe, c'mon, Bart, you know what day this is. I'm just sorry to see that you haven't vacated the ranch by now. So, we thought we'd make it official and tell you that you are now trespassing."

Bart spat on the ground as he approached the group on foot and replied, "Sorry Ben, but it is you guys that are trespassing. I'm not giving this land up. The DoA's case is full of holes, no matter what letters you write. I'd invite y'all in for some coffee, but I didn't put any on for such a large crowd. And, since you put it this way, I'm not too inclined to invite you in. Gonna have to ask you to leave and get off my land."

"Bart, we don't want any trouble now, so please get on quietly so nobody gets hurt. We'll give you to the end of the day to pack up your stuff and move on out. If you need to store stuff nearby before you can haul it all off, Meg in town will give you space to stash your stuff until you can haul it further away."

"Won't need to, not going, not now and not ever."

Ben introduced his accomplices, "this here is Sheriff Owens, from the State. He's come along to enforce the eviction. And over on this side is his deputy, Bruce. We'll be back in the morning, in force to take you in if you're still here, Bart. Sorry to put it this way to you, but you're not giving us any choice." He turned to his two accomplices and nodded to their car. They got in, Ben driving, and turned around on the narrow road and went on their way.

Well, that set the tone. They admitted their intention to take him by force. He felt justified to use force himself at this point.

He placed a call to his nephew Danny. "Hi, Danny, it's

Uncle Bart. How are you?"

"Good, Uncle Bart, how about you? Nice to hear from you."

"I'm calling to let you know what's going on here. As we discussed, the Feds are intending to evict me. Not gonna happen. I've put my will in a safe deposit box in Boise and mailed a key to you with information on getting in there. Also put a bunch of information in there on all the gear that's our here and the systems and all."

"Sounds serious, Uncle. What do you think is going to happen?"

"I don't intend to give up the property, Danny. But I'm not sure how it's going to work out. In the safe deposit box are also the legal docs, my lawyer's contact info. If they get me, you may be able to take up the fight and take what legal action my lawyer recommends. He's solidly on my side and he'd hate to see the Feds prevail in this."

"Geez, Uncle Bart, this sounds mighty serious. You need help there? I can be there tomorrow night, help you hold them off."

"No, no, the last thing I want is to put you in harm's way on this. Need you to take up the fight, press charges for trespassing and whatever they might think of doing to me. If this turns nasty, and it might, I'll feel good about having defended the land against the Feds, no matter what. As you know by now, I don't want to live with the thought that they could steal my land and get away with it. I'd rather go down fighting. If they shoot me, it'll be murder."

"Damn, I sure hope it doesn't come to that."

"Me too. I hope if we come to shooting at each other that they'll come to their senses and reconsider. You be good now. Love you lots and I think the whole world of you."

"Thanks, Uncle Bart. You be careful, you hear? I don't want to lose you. And thanks for having faith in me. I'll fight for that land. Need to keep it in the family."

"OK, Danny, you take care too. Hope to see you when

this is over." He disconnected. He fixed himself supper but he wasn't really hungry. Yet, he knew he better eat a good supper and a good breakfast. Might be a long day. As he ate, he couldn't help wonder if this was his last supper. *Hmmm, kind of lonely this last supper, compared to that famous one, about 2000 years ago.*

The next morning he rose early, brewed a strong pot of coffee, with lots to spare for his thermos to supply him for the rest of the day. His breakfast consisted of scrambled eggs with biscuits and ketchup and a dill pickle. He loved those big pickles, all nice and salty, even for breakfast.

After breakfast, he made the rounds on his water supply and generator, checked that all systems were up and functional and then drove in his buggy to where his Hummer was. He figured that was his best first defensive position. He just wasn't sure what they would bring to take him in.

Sure enough, just like clockwork, at 9:00 am they showed up, triggering the sensors at the entrance to his ranch property. He'd rigged a speaker with solar cells for power, about 300 feet from his entrance.

"Hold it right there, gentlemen, you are trespassing and any further movement onto my property will be met with resistance. Please turn around and leave, NOW," he spoke into the mike. The sound surprised them, not expecting to be seen and not expecting to be addressed out in the middle of nowhere, so to speak.

Sheriff Owens stepped out of his patrol car with a megaphone and shouted back, "Mr. Bowing, we've come to evict you from this property. We hope you'll come peacefully. As of yesterday, we consider you a trespasser on this property and will take you by force if necessary."

They had come with three patrol cars this time. Bart couldn't tell how many people were in the cars. He figured up to four per vehicle, meaning a total of 12.

"You know what the answer is. I'm not going to ask you but this once more to leave this property. I will not be responsible for any harm that might come to you if you persist. One more step and it's at your risk. Your move, Sheriff."

Sheriff Owens got back into his car and started to drive down the road. Bart had wished against all hope it wouldn't come to this, but he had decided long ago that he was committed to this path of action. He'd had the sheriff's car in the sights of the M-240B and he hesitated for a few more seconds. If he waited too long, he'd lose the opportunity to take out the car. He wanted at least two shots, just in case his calibration was off and he missed the first shot. His trigger finger was feeling hot as he started to squeeze. The burst of shots almost came as a surprise to Bart as well. He was almost in a trance, knowing that after this shot all hell would brake lose.

The sheriff's car exploded in a fireball and parts flew in all directions as the burst of bullets did their job. Bart was certain that nobody inside that car survived. He was hoping that Ben was not in there this time.

The other two cars came to an instant stop. They ran in reverse, trying to get around the corner, back towards the entrance. Bart was tempted to take out another car while he had the chance, but he had to give them the opportunity to call it off and get away. As long as they were vacating his property or making motions in that direction, they were not trespassing and he had to let them go.

Bart looked at the monitor with the cam at the entrance to verify that they were in deed leaving. But they didn't show up. *So, they decided to try something else,* he thought. OK, so be it. As he scanned his sensor panel, he confirmed that they had stopped someplace inside his property and moved out in two directions. Probably four people going right and four going left, according to his sensors.

Bart jumped into his buggy after he disabled the Hummer and the M-240B so they couldn't use it against him. He couldn't drive the Hummer where he had to go, so it was buggy and his M25 with the 10x/20xmm Bausch & Lomb scopes. He had it rigged with the dual scopes to provide flexibility. He didn't have the tripod for this one with him and the 20xmm scope needed some stabilization.

He drove around the knoll and up to the highpoint overlooking both sides of the main road. He could cover both approaches from there and his sniper rifle was just right for this job.

He had a good defensive position at the top, providing solid cover against rifle fire and approach by foot, but if they decided to mobilize heavy artillery, they could take him out with a good shot. He wasn't going to give them that chance.

He was in position, lying on his belly and looking in the direction of the sensors that were triggered. *There they were; didn't even think to wear camouflage.* They stood out in the terrain and made easy targets. They must not have figured on the level of his defenses and fire power. If he were in charge, Bart thought, he'd call this off and do a proper reconnaissance of the ranch and develop a proper assault.

Bart decided to take out the group on the left, figuring he could take them out with the semi-automatic rifle. He waited until all four of them were well away from trees, so that after the first shot they would need precious seconds to reach cover.

He lined up his first shot, already planning his second shot. The group on the right were out of sight at the moment and he didn't have to worry about them just yet.

He lined up the crosshairs in the 10x and squeezed the trigger. The shot rang out, echoing off the rocks as Bart quickly panned the rifle to his next victim. He saw his first bullet hit his mark. The second shot took out the next guy. The other two were getting close to trees for cover and Bart hurried his next shot. It missed. *Damn, precious seconds lost,* he thought. The third intended victim got behind a tree, but number four had the bad luck to stumble on a root or rock or something. Bart squeezed off another round and the man was history. Bart had only a brief moment to wonder if he made a widow or two today. Well, he couldn't dwell on that.

He had his third victim pinned behind that tree. From his vantage point, he could keep that spot covered while he attended to the group on the right. He shifted around and scanned for any movement in that direction.

He saw them scurrying from tree to tree, trying to gain some ground in his direction. The next guy that poked his head around a tree to see if the coast was clear was met with a bullet that hit the tree bark right next to his face. It didn't do any damage to him, but it surely got him the message that staying behind the tree would be a better idea.

Bart waited for several minutes, scanning right and left to make sure nobody beat a retreat to mount an assault from another direction. The minutes dragged on and soon it was half an hour during which nobody made a move.

He decided to take the offensive and get this thing over with. He didn't really want to shoot any more guys. He hoped that they would get some sense and call it off. He figured if he could get behind the four guys on the right, the only one left on the left side would give up as well.

Bart made sure nobody was peeking and slipped back down behind his hill. He scrambled down a ravine that led around to the right, towards the entrance side of his property. It gave good cover and was not easily seen from the road. He was pretty sure that the guys could not see it either from where they were. He reached the spot where he would turn to his left and then approach the intruders from behind and below. At this point, the brush gave him cover. He could see all four of them sitting on the ground with their backs to the trees. Bart wondered if they were waiting for reinforcements to arrive. That wouldn't be good in his current position. If they arrived right now, he'd be caught in between the original group and the reinforcements.

He gauged his distance to the intruders to be about 100 feet, give or take. That was plenty close for him to plug his targets. He decided to stay under cover. He unpacked his mini megaphone and called out to them: "Gentlemen, I think this show is over. I have you all covered ..." One of the guys started to move as if to scramble around his tree to regain cover. "HOLD IT!" Bart yelled, "One more inch and I'll shoot."

The guy froze in mid motion and then slowly stood up and raised his hands over his head in surrender.

"I suggest that all of you drop your weapons and move down the hill they way you came up. I've got ordnance coverage set up that will take you out if I chose." The latter was a lie, but Bart hoped that his display of preparedness and willingness to use force would convince them that he was telling the truth.

"I will meet you at the road to escort you out. Your weapons will be taken care of and the Department will get them back. You won't be needing them any more today."

One of them yelled back, "What about the sheriff's car and the other guys you took out?" What's going to happen to their bodies?"

"I'll arrange for a peaceful party to come and get them. I doubt that anyone survived that explosion of the sheriff's car." Actually he hoped that was true. Nobody had had time to go and check on the wreck. He would do that as soon as he saw his "guests" on their way.

======================

Waking up to yet another mass shooting this morning, my heart aches for the families of those who lost someone, and for the injured. And, my mind rages in anger because as a society we don't give a rat's patootie about the mass killings or even the single killings going on in America. We have become squeamish, we have become a bunch of wimps. In other words, we don't have the stomach to enforce our own laws. It is more important to us that we do not look like a bunch of "savages" because we administered severe punishment.

A recent article in the newspaper lamented that solitary confinement was too cruel. While that article cites some questionable reasons for confining a prisoner to solitary, it is in general tune with many prisoner rights advocates. What we seem to forget is that the function of punishment is to punish, not to coddle, cater to and provide the comforts of normal life to prisoners.

Along with that debate is that the death penalty is too severe. We should abolish it, the argument goes, because too many innocent suspects are wrongfully executed. Just stop and think about that for a moment. Will the abolition of the death penalty prevent the wrongful detainer of a suspect? Hardly. The issue of wrongfully convicting an innocent person is something that needs to be addressed, regardless of whether we have a death penalty or not. Granted, abolishing the death penalty would prevent executing the wrong person, however, my point is this: Imposing the death penalty with certainty and speed will reduce the number of crimes requiring the death penalty to be administered significantly, if not to zero. And, the less crimes there are, the less wrongfully accused persons there will be.

We have come to a sad state of affairs in this country. We do not have crime prevention as a priority. We really do not care whether people are robbed, raped or killed. Oh sure, we moan and wring our hands in woe whenever there is a new report of a killer gone wild and mowing down several people, or a young girl is abducted and raped. We don't even do that when we read about a burglary or some kind of theft and other "minor" crimes. Despite the rash of killings, rapes, robberies and other crimes, we simply refuse to do the right thing to prevent crimes. If we did, the number of crimes would plummet drastically. One of the hottest topics in this subject is crime prevention and gun control. Gun control in the sense of limiting to the point of total prohibition, the ability of citizens to keep and bear arms.

I think the scariest movie that I ever saw was "The Minority Report" wherein a group of specially gifted women were used to predict forthcoming crimes. They had the talent to visualize a crime that was contemplated by a particular perpetrator. The police then used these predictions to rush to the scene and intervene in the execution of the crime and arresting the would-be criminal. This may sound so very useful in reducing the number of crimes committed. And, sure enough, reality tends to follow fiction. One hears more and more about crime "prevention" with the noble goal to stop crime before it is committed. Psychologists are engaged in analyzing people's behavior with the goal of identifying a high potential for some criminal action. Behavior patterns are reviewed with the goal of establishing some rules for defining a would-be criminal before the act.

This concept may sound wonderful; it will reduce crime by intercepting the would-be criminal before he or she can act. Yet, that concept is frightening because of the potential for error and the implication of behavior control. It fosters in an age where the government will decide what constitutes proper behavior and what is considered subversive or otherwise "incorrect." Memories of George Orwell's novel *1984* come to mind, where the government, represented by Big Brother, controls all aspects of individual life in an attempt to control the behavior and the thoughts of individuals. Incidentally, that book I would classify as the scariest novel I have read because George Orwell was right in his predictions that he fictionalized in that novel. His timing was simply off by many decades. Perhaps a better title might have been *2084*. But, that is the topic of another discussion in this collection.

As we hear about more and more killings and mass murders in America, the police and other investigators, along with the media, try to figure out if the crimes could have been foreseen and thus prevented. The "experts" try to figure out what the behavior pattern was during the time leading up to the crime. All this is with the focus of trying to figure out who might be planning to commit a crime, such as murder.

Our Founding Fathers, in the framing of the Constitution and the fourth Amendment, provided that people would be answerable for crimes only upon indictment of a Grand Jury. This is essentially the "people are considered innocent until proven guilty" doctrine. I think in their wisdom the Founding Fathers saw the potential danger of considering someone guilty before they are proven to be so in a court of law. All this talk about trying to predetermine someone's intentions in the hope of preventing a crime are of course in direct conflict with this right to be considered innocent until proven guilty. How can you be guilty of something you haven't committed yet? How can you be convicted without the indictment of a Grand Jury?

Another focus of crime prevention is the control or restriction of access to guns and ammunition. The "the right of the people to keep and bear arms" in this country was guaranteed by the founders of this great nation in the Second Amendment to the Constitution. The thing that is important to remember about the Second Amendment was the reasoning behind granting this right: the necessity of a "well regulated Militia' to provide for the security of a free State." Despite the use of the term "well regulated", and without stipulating who would do the regulating, one must come to the conclusion that this amendment was written to guarantee a right, not to impose a duty. And most of the American people have defended this right, in spite of numerous attempts by our government to infringe upon this right, in direct violation of the supreme law of this land.

Let us examine the reasoning for including this right in the Constitution. The Founding Fathers knew from bitter experience that it is so easy for a government to overstep its purpose and to enslave its citizens. They knew that power corrupts and that the governors will soon attempt to rule the governed. In the Federalist Papers and in the Antifederalist papers they repeatedly pointed out the need for the governed to be able to control the governors and to be able to kick the government out of office when they overstep their limited purpose.

On this subject, Alexander Hamilton wrote in *The Federalist No. 28*:

> "We should recollect that the extent of the military force must, at all events, be regulated by the resources of the country. For a long time to come, it will not be possible to maintain a large army; and as the means of doing this increase, the population and natural strength of the community will proportionally increase. When will the time arrive that the federal government can raise and maintain an army capable of erecting a despotism over the great body of the people of an immense empire, who are in a situation, through the medium of their State governments, to take measures for their own defense, with all the celerity, regularity, and system of independent nations? "

What he is addressing is the need for the people, through their close ties to their State governments, to be able to control the Federal government, through the use of force, if necessary. Towards this end, the Second Amendment was adopted which includes the right of all citizens to keep and bear arms. There was at the time, a great fear that the proposed form of government would usurp its purpose and limits with the result of "enslaving the people" just as King George of Britain had done. They were set on preventing a recurrence of that oppression. How have we fared in the mean time? This is discussed further under the topic of "Big

Brother".

James Madison wrote in *The Federalist No. 51*:

> "If men were angels, no government would be necessary. If angels were to govern men, neither external nor internal controls on government would be necessary. In framing a government which is to be administered by men over men, the great difficulty lies in this: you must first enable the government to control the governed; and in the next place oblige it to control itself. A dependence on the people is, no doubt, the primary control on the government; but experience has taught mankind the necessity of auxiliary precautions.

This also addresses the fear of the federal government overstepping its bounds and the need to have in place the means to reign in those who would govern the nation. These auxiliary precautions that Madison refers to are the ability of the people to bear arms to prevent the Federal government from becoming too powerful. I think this concept scares the hell out of many people. The idea of another armed revolution in this country seems unfathomable. We are way too comfortable, yet, to consider armed revolt against our federal government. And yet, that is exactly what our Founding Fathers recommended. When the governed feel that their government is too oppressive, they must throw it out and establish a new government. The idea of a new revolution would scare most people because they would fear for their possessions, their livelihood and their very lives in such an upheaval. But that is exactly what the colonists considered and they decided that it was all worthwhile to throw off the shackles of Britain's government.

Now, I am not suggesting that we start a revolution in this country. We are not at that stage. However, we must retain the ability to do so. We must be able to hold that threat over our government in order to control it. Our Founding Fathers insisted on it; they knew what power will do to people and they foresaw the potential tyranny of even a representative government. That is the primary reason they insisted on the Second Amendment.

Alas, our federal government has seen the threat to their continuation as governors. They have taken steps to water down this right to keep and bear arms.

The word infringement, as I used it above in relation to guns, implies any restrictions or limitations. That also means that the type of arms that citizens may keep and bear must not be infringed. The founders did not stipulate that these arms shall be limited to just one weapon, nor to just one type of weapon. There is still a lot of talk about banning ordinary citizens from owning assault weapons. This seems to me to be totally ludicrous in light of the simple, unrestricted right granted by the Second Amendment. As it is written, the Second Amendment even allows citizens to own tanks, rocket launchers and any other weapon that will keep an unwanted federal government at bay.

Alas, when you think about it, we obviously have long ago given up our ability to defend ourselves from the government. Therefore, we are now slaves to our government, albeit that the government has, so far, been reasonably benevolent.

But, back to crimes and guns. It seems that the fear of crimes with guns is what drives some people to support limiting the right to bear arms. The subject of gun control arises after every notorious shooting spree or other assault with guns. We apparently figure that if we can keep guns out of the hands of ordinary citizens that we can prevent crimes. So, under the auspices of crime prevention, we try to take guns out of the would-be killers' hands in the hopes that the crime will not be possible. Are we all so naïve that we think people who are inclined to commit a crime are going to respect the law that limits access to guns? All we accomplish is to make it difficult for law-abiding citizens to obtain guns while doing nothing that is effective to prevent criminals from obtaining guns. The fact that citizens with the right to carry guns have stopped criminals in the past doesn't seem to carry much weight. Thus we foster an environment of crime.

As I stated above, by our actions we demonstrate that we don't really care whether crimes are committed. If we did, we would administer our laws as they were intended. Take our death penalty, for example. While there are many murderers on death row, for some reason it takes decades to carry out a sentence. If we sentenced killers and rapists to death and carried out the executions more swiftly, within months or one year at the most, the number of killings and rapes would drop so drastically that we would all be surprised when a crime is actually committed. This is an absolute guarantee.

Consider this: All of our actions are driven by one thing and one thing only. That is the risk/reward ratio. In other words what's in it for me and what does it cost me? As long as the cost of crime is low, crime will be committed. I can't help wonder why this is such a difficult concept to understand?

John Locke, the famous philosopher of the 18th century observed: "Good and evil, reward and punishment, are the only motives to a rational creature: these are the spur and reins whereby all mankind are set on work, and guided." As I said, we are motivated by our personal risk/reward ratio.

To get a clearer focus on this behavior, consider how you make your daily decisions on everything from what to wear today, to which way to drive to work today, to what to buy, and even whether to swipe that little item from the store counter without paying for it. You engage the risk/reward analysis and make a decision prior to every action you take.

How many of you refrain from stealing because you don't want to be embarrassed if caught or go to prison? Those who are not afraid to steal, do so in the belief that either they'll get away with it or, if caught, the punishment, if any, won't be all that bad.

Unfortunately, there is one big obstacle in the way of administering justice quickly. If we did carry out sentences quickly, we would put a whole bunch of lawyers out of work. It is in their interest that we continue the legal wranglings and procrastinations for as long as possible. And, since more than half of our lawmakers are lawyers, we have a fat chance of getting that changed.

Next, take the case of insanity. As you surely know from the news, insanity is a plea that is used more often than not in the hopes of getting the sentence reduced. After all, the poor perpetrator didn't know what he or she was doing and thus shouldn't be held accountable for their actions. After all, we, as a humanitarian society, don't want to be too harsh here. There are numerous examples of the killer being caught red handed, in full view of many witnesses. And still, we need to conduct lengthy trials and appeals on the basis of some excuse, such as insanity. Who benefits from the dragged out insanity pleas? You guessed it, the attorneys; and the perpetrator who might just get away with the crime.

I guarantee you that if we refused to accept insanity as a plea for clemency, the number of insanity pleas would drop by at least 90%. The few remaining cases of valid insanity should still not be accepted as a license to kill. If you are insane and commit a crime, that's too bad. You're done. Consider the punishment of execution as an incurable consequence of your sickness. In truth, I don't think that truly clinically insane people commit crimes. What we try to defend as insanity in the case of murder is more likely enraged, blind, unthinking reaction to some condition that drives the killer into action. I am convinced that if the result of such "insane" behavior were swift and definite punishment, the would-be killer would manage to come to his or her senses and stop short of committing the murder.

You might wonder how I can make these claims. As a world traveler, I have witnessed different societies and seen the results of their policies. The most striking example is Saudi Arabia.

As you may know, people who are caught stealing lose a hand as punishment. Can you imagine the number of one-handed people in this country if we adopted such a policy? Yet there are extremely few people without a hand in Saudi Arabia. Why? The answer is very simple: The punishment is known and it is administered. Period! There is no doubt, there are no lawyers trying to get things changed for ever and ever through legal processes. There is simply no need. Crime is practically nonexistent.

I spent a couple of 2-week stays for business in Saudi Arabia and this is what happened. I had just recently purchased my first 35 mm SLR camera with lenses and attachments and filters; big bucks, all nicely tucked into a short attaché-like case. I took it along to do some touristy picture taking as time permitted. However, I didn't want to drag it along with me to the business meetings. Now, the dilemma was this: My hotel room door didn't latch, the lock was broken. Not only that, but it was hung crooked so that it opened all the way. I could not close the door. At night I used a chair to keep it closed. So, what to do with my expensive camera outfit? Actually it was not a problem. I had heard that stealing is not tolerated in this country. I just left it there on the desk by the window, in full view from the hallway. I had no doubt that it would be there at night when I returned. WOW! Can you imagine such peace of mind in America?

There are many money changers in Saudi Arabia, accommodating the various foreigners with their money changing needs. The one we were using had his place of business in a store window that was open to the sidewalk and closed off on the inside. Where the window would have been there was a rolling shutter secured at night with a tiny brass hasp lock. Judging by the number of drawers full of various bills, there must have been several hundred thousand dollars worth of currency in that window and all that kept the would-be thieves away was a tiny brass lock. That money was as secure as the gold in Fort Knox, I'd wager.

Another example was an incident I created at a restaurant. At that time, food was not exactly great and there was only one reasonable restaurant in town. It was the top restaurant by local standards and the food was not bad. I ordered a goulash and rice dish. The waiter brought it without the gravy but ladled the gravy onto the rice at the table, two tablespoons of it. I like my gravy and I want the rice swimming in it. So I asked him for more gravy, which he was glad to provide. Two days later, we ate there again and I ordered the same dish. Same routine, two tablespoons of gravy. So, in my inimitable diplomatic style I asked the waiter why he only ladles two spoonfuls of gravy on the rice. That was about the worst thing I could have done. You see, what happened is that I inadvertently questioned his integrity. I had great difficulty trying to console the poor guy that everything was alright for the rest of the evening. It was simply his mindset, perhaps brought on by a society that does not tolerate crime and dishonesty. Now this might seem a bit draconian, but if a society realizes that certain behavior, such as theft, murder, rape and so on is not acceptable and will not be tolerated, then that society will come to grips with that morality. This would be so even if the acceptability of that behavior is communicated via punishment for engaging in the unacceptable behavior.

I am convinced that the prospect, even the fear, of swift punishment is a very effective deterrent to crime, as the Saudi Arabian examples seem to confirm. As I stated above, if we took punishment for crimes seriously and carried out the sentences more swiftly, the number of killings and rapes would drop so drastically that we would all be surprised when a crime is actually committed. This is an absolute guarantee. We could then convert many of our prisons into hotels or resorts or offices (with some internal remodeling of course).

As a society, we have to decide whether we will indeed surrender our lives, properties and pursuits of happiness to our government or not. And we must decide whether crime is acceptable or not. I'm afraid that we have long ago decided to surrender to our government.

With respect to gun control, which I have said is unconstitutional, I have a solution as well. Allow people to own and bear (read carry) any guns they chose. But, if you are caught committing a crime with a gun you get executed if you fired it and life imprisonment without parole if you merely used it as a threat. I absolutely guarantee that the number of shootings would all but disappear in this country.

Separation of Church & State

He was all pumped up. This was going to be THE game. Miller High and Jute High had been arch rivals for as long as both were in existence and at the moment their record was tied. This game obviously meant a lot to both teams. Robert's girlfriend, Ginny, noticed how pent up he was. "You ought to let it go Rob. I'm not going to say 'it's only a game' because I know better, but I've never seen you so tight before a game."

"Don't tell me to let it .." he started to reply in a hot temper, "geez, you're right. Listen to me jump back at you. I'm sorry. I need to cool off and do my meditation. You mind if I call it a night?"

"It's OK, I understand. When will I see you?"

"Tomorrow, before the game as usual, I'll pick you up." He drove Ginny home. "Thanks for understanding," he said as he kissed her good night. "G'night, I love you so very much, Babe. Thanks for being here for me."

Robert was a serious Christian. You wouldn't call him devout because he didn't attend church on a regular basis, but he had found the Lord early on in his life. He could remember praying every night in bed before he shut his mind off to find sleep, "Dear God, please protect my family and keep them safe, and please don't let the house burn down." He wasn't sure where his concern for the fire came from, but it was a regular part of his prayer as a young boy. His family never went to church and his religious upbringing was nil at the time. His exposure to religion came when he joined the Boy Scouts. It was expected to go to church and the troop met in the church activity hall.

Because he had several friends whose families were regular church goers, he tagged along for the social benefits of his friends. That's how he came to learn about God and Jesus and what it meant to be a Christian. It struck a tune with him and he fully embraced Christianity just before his Confirmation. He was 14 at the time.

Now, in his later teens, he had come to rely on God's presence and knew that He would answer prayers. Robert and God had a regular dialog going; Robert just knew that God was there and that He would keep him safe as long as he didn't do anything totally foolish.

The night before every game, he would go into his meditation to ask for God's blessings on the coming game and to keep him out of harm, to inspire him to do his utmost and to help him focus on the game's plays. Before each game, on the field, he and his team mates would gather in a big circle and pray for a few moments, ending with a great "Amen!" as they threw their hands in the air.

Lately, some guy in the audience started to object to these displays of their faith. He even filed for an injunction with the courts. It was truly irritating. To Robert and his team mates, this was an important ritual. They were all in on it, even though some of his team mates were Muslim and some were Jewish. Some were even agnostic, they didn't believe in God or a god of any kind. But, they went along with the prayer circle in the name of team spirit.

Robert had asked Chet about it. Chet was a confirmed

nonbeliever. "So, why do you go along with our prayer circle on the field, Chet? I know you don't believe and you know you don't have to join the circle"

"It amuses me to hear what you guys are praying about. And, besides, we are a team and we do all things together. If it makes the rest of the guys feel good to pray before the game, I'm cool with that. It's no skin off my back in any case," he said with a grin. So, it had become a firm and important ritual for the team. To hear people in the stands object to it was a shame. It put a cloud over that process, but the team was committed.

Tonight, Robert was more tense than normally though. That guy Robberson, Stuart was his first name, was making a pest out of himself. He'd been more and more vocal at every game lately and Robert was agitated about it. He was determined to let him have it if he made any noise about their prayer tomorrow.

The following day, after his normal game day breakfast of scrambled eggs with salsa and a 16 oz. steak, Robert jumped into his car and drove by Ginny's house to pick her up. She was so beautiful that Robert gave thanks to God every time he saw her. It was just a fleeting little "Thank you God for bringing Ginny into my life" prayer. He had these quick little "chats" with God throughout the day. It was part of his direct connection to God.

They drove to the stadium and he told Ginny that he'll see her after the game. During the game there was little time to spend with her, even though she always had a seat at the 50 yard line on their side.

They had gotten through their usual pre-game locker room routine. Coach Jones gave his usual pep talk and expressed his confidence that all the players would be focused on the moment. He never reviewed plays and ran though the game book on game day. That was done during the week and every player was expected to be prepared for this game. It was part of Coach Jones' method and it kept the anxiety out of the players. We all had that special confidence that came with knowing that each player knew his job.

It was time to get back out on the field. They had already done their exercises and practice runs and passes. Elroy and Leroy had done their kicking warm ups. As the team ran out between the cheer leaders onto mid-field, they formed their circle as usual. When they were all assembled, they laid their hands on the shoulders of their neighbors and Robert, as team captain started the prayer, "Dear Lord, we gather once again…"

"STOP THAT!" came the cry over a megaphone. It was that guy Robberson. This time he brought a megaphone so he would be heard more easily.

Robert started over, "Dear Lord, we gather once again by your grace to partake in this sport that we love so much. We ask…"

"I WANT THAT PRAYER STOPPED THIS INSTANT! THIS IS A PUBLIC SCHOOL AND THERE SHALL BE NO PRAYER ON PUBLIC PORPERTY," Robberson shouted.

Robert had had enough. He said to the team, "Stand by, guys, I'll be back. Please keep the circle for now." With that, Robert disengaged from the circle and headed for the bench. The ref was standing there and Robert asked if he could borrow his mike for a moment.

"Well, I don't know, Robert," the ref said, not sure how to handle this situation. But he always liked Robert and had great respect for him. He unclipped his mike and handed it to Robert.

"Look, Mr. Robberson, I know where you are coming from and I respect your concern about separation of Church and State, and all that," he spoke into the mike. His voice carried throughout the stadium. "But what we have here is not a separation of Church and State issue. Just because we are in a public school and want to pray, does not mean that Congress has passed a law establishing a particular religion. We have team members in our prayer circle from various religious and even non-religious backgrounds. As a team we find that our prayer circle is beneficial to us and a part of our collective religious preferences. Now, the Constitution of the United States, in the Second Amendment, specifically states that Congress shall protect the exercise of religion among the people of this country. That is what we are doing, exercising our religion. And the fact that the Constitution protects this right of ours, requires you to respect that right as well. You are not anointed or even appointed to prescribe to us when, where and how we may exercise our religious observances. If this turns you off and truly offends you, you have the right to ignore our prayer session; nobody is asking you to take part in it. But, we beg your indulgence for a few moments while we "do our thing". I'm sure you can tune us out for a few moments. If that is so very difficult, perhaps you can take a few minutes to go to the food stand and get your self a drink or hot dog or something. Now, we are going to go on with our normal routine."

A spontaneous roar went up from the team in their circle and moments later, was picked up by the crowd in the stadium. Robert handed the mike back to the ref and said, "Thanks, Joe, I owe you one, very much obliged." As Robert returned to the circle his agitation over the issue melted away as he savored the roar of the crowd. He rejoined the circle and resumed his prayer. Robberson's megaphone remained quiet. After the "Amen" and raised hands, he walked back to the sideline and glanced at Robberson. His dark expression told Robert that this was not the end of it, but he felt great for the shot across the bow that he had sent him.

=====================

One of the recurring topics in the news is the separation of Church and State. The argument is made that the Constitution requires a separation of Church and State. Upon reading the First Amendment to the Constitution without emotion or predisposed feelings about what it says, you will notice that the Constitution absolutely does not require there to be a separation of Church and State. What it does say is that "Congress shall make no law respecting an establishment of religion, or prohibiting the free exercise thereof." As Justice Anthony Kennedy wrote in one of his opinions regarding this matter:

> The bottom line, Justice Anthony M. Kennedy wrote, is that "the Constitution does not oblige government to avoid any public acknowledgment of religion's role in society."

We hear about it when someone is upset about a cross on public land, such as the one in Providence, Rhode Island, the memorials to Utah Highway Patrolmen, or the one in the Mojave Desert in southern California, even though it has stood there for decades. Or we hear that someone decides that the Christian heritage of a particular county is no reason to show a cross in the county's logo, such as Los Angeles County. There are cases of the Ten Commandments being displayed in a high school in Virginia and in some courthouses. We continue to hear about sports teams or cheer leaders who want to show their religious zeal at school games, only to have some one individual object on the basis that it, being a public school, is indication of the government endorsing a religion. There is a general uproar made by some groups of people, generally small, special interest groups or even individuals over these public displays of religion.

I do not know of any laws in existence which establish a religion. Displaying the Ten Commandments (which by the way, are an original Jewish document, not Christian. and the Qur'an makes reference to most of those commandments as well, so we have an ecumenical situation in this case) in front of a court house, allowing a county to include a cross in its emblem, mentioning "under God" in our pledge, supporting religious organizations through monetary gifts and tax breaks, etc. etc. do not in any way establish a law. In stead, these things, if they are continued to be allowed, exemplify the free exercise of religion, as guaranteed by the Constitution. This guarantee surely extends even to public agencies and governments. Suppressing these rights directly tramples on our supreme law, the Constitution, and is evidence of laws being passed that in effect establish a religion, that is, a non-religion, or at least establish laws that prohibit or restrict the free exercise of religion.

Fellowship of Christian Athletes: Spokesperson Dal Shealy said that the court's ruling (barring prayer at Santa Fe's public school events) is "a bizarre and ironic intrusion...While we're seeing the blossoming of spiritual life among the nation's athletes, our highest court has shown barren hostility to all thing[s] religious in public life. [The Fellowship of Christian Athletes] has one warning for the Supreme Court: "If we choose to remove truly positive influences, such as prayer, from our schools, we must no longer be perplexed when appalling tragedies become increasingly and disturbingly common." One could consider this somewhat prophetic, judging by the increased violence of our younger generations.

It puzzles me on what basis a particular parent wants to stop a sports team from praying on the field. It is their right; you don't have to pray along with them, just show a bit of patience and tolerance for their right to do so. If it offends you to see them kneeling and bowing their heads, turn around for a moment, read the program, tune out, get a hot dog or whatever you want so you don't' have to endure the "indignity" of watching someone display their devotion to that morality that our Founding Fathers found so important to the survival of this nation.

Just as all have a right to practice their religion, or not, you have a right not to participate. But, you do NOT have a right to prevent the exercise of someone else's right.

There is a challenge to drawing the line between government accommodation of religion versus laws regarding the establishment of religion. One might gain significant insight into the thinking of our Founding Fathers by reading the Federalist Papers and the Antifederalist Papers. Therein one will find the reasoning for the way the Constitution is framed and therein the authors discussed their fears and assumptions. One of the recurring themes was that they felt that a civilization will be best served if it adheres to morality and the principles promoted by "Christian" tenets.

Some quotes from our early Presidents, congressmen, judges and signers of the Declaration of Independence and the Constitution may help to add perspective of why the Christian influence is so strong in this country and why they tried to make sure that that influence be protected.

> George Washington, first President of the United States: "It is the duty of all nations to acknowledge the providence of Almighty God, to obey His will, to be grateful for His benefits, and humbly to implore His protection and favor."

Seems to be an endorsement of religious principles to enhance the success of a nation.

> John Adams, second President of the United States: "We have no government armed with power capable of contending with human passions unbridled by morality and religion. Our Constitution was made only for a moral and religious people. It is wholly inadequate to the government of any other."

What he is saying is that this is a nation founded on religious principles. He also indicates that this Constitution, i.e. our form of government, was made for a moral and religious people. They knew that government by representation still needs moral people lest they ignore the basic tenets of Christianity and turn to despotism. While these Founding Fathers and many, many colonists who fought for our independence would like to see the continuation of religious principles, they made sure to leave the door open to other religions. They made sure that the right to practice religion, or not, would be protected by the supreme law of our land. Keep also in mind that at that time, the vast majority of religious people in America were Christians. The influx of Jews and Muslims and others came later.

Thomas Jefferson, third President of the United States: "And can the liberties of a nation be thought secure when we have removed their only firm basis, a conviction in the minds of the people that these liberties are of the gift of God? That they are not to be violated but with His wrath?"

What Jefferson was saying is that the violation of the religious principles upon which this nation was built would incur the wrath of God. If you don't believe in God, whether He is Hebrew, Islam, Christian, Hindu or any other, you can interpret Jefferson's warning that the principles are good and they are the basis for a free society.

Jedediah Morse, Patriot and Educator: "To the kindly influence of Christianity we owe that degree of civil freedom and political and social happiness which mankind now enjoys. Wherever the pillars of Christianity shall be overthrown, our present form of republican forms of government – and all blessings which come from them – must fall with them."

What Morse is saying to us is that the solid foundation of our republican form of government is the influence of Christian principles. And he gives us fair warning that the overthrow of Christianity will spell the end of a free America.

> James Wilson, Original Justice of the U.S. Supreme Court: "Human law must rest its authority ultimately upon the authority of that law which is Divine. Far from being rivals or enemies, religion and law are twin sisters, friends and mutual assistants. Indeed, these two sciences run into each other."

This is another endorsement that religious principles, such as Christian doctrine are needed to protect the freedoms that we enjoy.

> Joseph Story, U.S. Supreme Court Justice: "One of the beautiful boasts of our municipal jurisprudence is that Christianity is a part of the Common Law. There never has been a period in which Common Law did not recognize Christianity as lying at its foundations. I verily believe Christianity necessary to the support of civil society."

This clearly claims that a civil society, one which respects the rights of its people, requires the inclusion of Christian principles in the law of the land.

I think it is important to keep in mind that when our Founding Fathers referred to "Christian" principles, they may have meant Christianity specifically, as that was the majority of their persuasion. However, a review of various religions will show an uncanny similarity between them. They all proscribe essentially the same moral principles of love and respect for all mankind, to do no harm to others, to refrain from stealing and murder, to honor your father and mother, just to name a few.

The ironic thing is that it is exactly the Christian principles that the critics love to attack which are the foundation of their ability and right to criticize those principles. Like it or not, the morality of our society and the foundation of our laws are built on religious principles. We have 35 million laws on the books written to enforce the 10 Commandments.

With regard to the Ten Commandments, also referred to as the Decalogue, as mentioned above, the prescriptions are first of all from Hebrew Scripture, later adopted by Christians. The prescriptions are also referred to in the Islamic Qur'an. Thus any objection to them on the basis of the establishment of a religion are unfounded. The fact that we adopt the readily recognized version of the Christian Bible is surely protected under the First Amendment that guarantees us (that is we, as a society and a civilization) the free exercise of our religion.

It is also ironic that the objections to public display of religion are likely to cause Congress to pass laws specifically to allow religious expression in public, in protection of the free exercise of religion. Those laws would make it more clear what the First Amendment means, for those who just don't get it.

As the quotations above indicate, Christianity was considered a central part of our society. At the time, the majority of the citizens of the American Colonies were Christian. As time passed by, over the last couple of centuries, the makeup of our society has changed considerably. We have a significant group of Hebrews, Moslems, Hindus, atheists, agnostics and others besides the majority of Christians. Up to this point, Congress has held the restriction of the First Constitutional Amendment by not passing any laws establishing a specific religion. It has continued, for the most part, to protect the right of citizens to pursue whatever religion, if any, they chose. Although, there are instances, such as Santa Fe's ban on prayer in public schools, that are local, rather than federal examples.

I came across a posting on the internet recently that summarizes this rather nicely:

> (Referring to the First Amendment) "It's called the establishment clause not the separation clause.

> "From my simple perspective and I think in the context of the actual events of the time (1770s) religious freedom meant that no State in the Union under the Constitution could force, by law, any citizen to participate in, confess, or otherwise practice any particular State sanctioned or preferred religion (A state religion). It would also forbid the creation of a State religion with attendant threats of incarceration or imposition of any punishment upon said citizens.

> "The objective of these freedoms was to allow citizens to believe what they wanted with no interference from the State as well as guarantee that States not mandate one religion, or sect within a religion, over another.

> "From that point going forward governments across the land, from municipal to federal, acknowledged God, His laws, and many other events and rituals of the Christian faith (and others) with little or no dissent. That all

changed in the late 1940's when the US Supreme Court violated the Constitution by interfering in the rights of the sovereign states and prohibiting the free exercise of religion."

His last sentence is pointing at a sad truth, which the critics of religious displays in public would likely celebrate. At the request of a few critics, the Supreme Court decided that religious freedom was not important any more. The feelings of a few dissenters was more important than the morality of the nation.

Perhaps, as one comic on the internet put it: "Concerning the Ten Commandments in courthouses and legislatures: You cannot post 'Thou Shalt Not Steal,' 'Thou Shalt Not Commit Adultery,' and 'Thou Shalt Not Lie' in a building full of lawyers, judges and politicians...It creates a hostile work environment."

Race

It was going to be a big day. He was all pumped up for the Afro Convention in DC. He had his speech prepared long ago and had been practicing it daily. Abraham Smithe had founded the Afro Convention, or ACon, as it was popularly called, about ten years ago and had been head of it ever since. He was a minister in SE Washington but that gave him plenty of time to work on ACon projects.

His parents had come to America from Jamaica in the '50s, before he had been born. They settled in Washington, DC where Abraham Mohammad Smithe was born to the delight of his parents. According to their stories, he had always been a showman from his early years. Abraham delighted in the attention of relatives, friends, schoolmates and whoever was around to watch his antics. Their focus on him gave him a rush as far back as he could remember. So, entering the ministry and serving a congregation was a natural ambition for him.

The morning started off with a beautiful sunrise splaying bright red color over the vast canopy of wispy clouds. Although the cherry blossoms had bloomed and gone,

WHAT'S WRONG IN AMERICA?

the trees showed that bright Spring green of new foliage. When you looked up at the sky, the leaves just glowed in their bright green luminescence with the blue sky backdrop. Abraham was always tempted to take yet another photograph. But, today he decided he had enough pictures of scenery and he wanted to get on with the day.

Following breakfast, he donned his iconic, dark blue three-piece suit with the narrow-pin stripes, white vest and red bow tie. He had never given a public speech without wearing this combination as far back as he could remember, even before the ACon days. The one variation he allowed himself were his shoes. Sometimes he'd wear the white spats, sometimes he'd wear black patent leather shoes, and sometimes he'd wear white shoes. It was a matter of comfort and how he felt that day. Today it was a pair of white shoes.

When he arrived at the Mall in his limo, driven by his chauffeur, David, he saw that all seemed to be set up. They had gotten permission to set up a stage near the Mall's East end, just West of 4th Street. That provided one of the longer blocks on the Mall; it was unbroken until 7th Street. Additional speakers had been set up on the sides of the Mall about the mid-point, near 6th Street. David had dropped him off in front of the National Art Galley on Madison Drive. Abraham slipped behind and below the stage where they had the usual Green Room set up.

The crowd had started to gather last night, with people camping out and using their sleeping bags. They wanted the prime spots near the stage. Judging by past conventions, this was going to be on the light side. He'd noticed a general decline in his audiences. Abraham wasn't sure why the decline. Maybe they needed to hear a different message; something new and fresh. He had been feeling a bit stale lately, even though he got pumped up for each event. However, today's speech was set, he couldn't change it at this stage. Abraham did not believe in ad-libbing; he always practiced his speeches so that he could stay on script and handle minor interruptions and distractions.

It was time to get on stage and do his thing. The Black Bees had done their musical act to get the crowd into a loose and lively mood. As Abraham came on stage he could immediately see that the Bees had done their job. The crowd was swaying and stomping even though the music had ceased. He also noticed that a good 90% of the crowd was made up of black people. That was to be expected.

As he approached the podium, the crowd raised a growing cheer to acknowledge his appearance. He put on his normal crowd facing smile, his teeth showing glistening white, and combined with his intense smiling eyes, he became a presence that reached far beyond the stage. From his experience, he judged the crowd to number between eight and twelve thousand. Less than in the past, but still a good showing.

He raised his arms to form a broad V, pumping his hands up and down. As the crowd roared more and more, he stretched his arms to the extreme, held his hands steady and then in a slow motion lowered his arms and ended with a final punch into the air with his right arm. It was a well known ritual and the crowd hushed to silence as he lowered his arm again. Abraham felt the adrenalin rush as he relished this little display of crowd control. He had their attention, to be sure.

He waited a few seconds to let the silence sink in and then he began: "My fellow Americans, I am so pleased to see you here today. Your presence sends a strong message to the men and women behind me in that big white building." He motioned to the Capitol behind the stage. "It says that we will not be ignored, that we will be heard and that we will not go away!"

The crowd reacted to that with renewed cheering, hand clapping and fist pumping.

He continued, "Now," he waited for the noise to settle, "there are those who want us to go away, to melt into the crowd of Americans, without distinction or recognition who we are. You may have seen the campaign by that guy Arlo Siccal trying to eliminate the racial questions in the census, job applications, hospital records, voting registrations, and on and on. He claims that if we do away with those questions and the answers, that racism will disappear in this country. He claims that as long as anyone is interested in the color of your skin that we will have racism in this country."

"Noooooooo! Never!" came the reply from the crowd.

"My friends, you are so right. It's not going to happen. We are black and we want the world to know it. We have suffered long and hard in this country at the hands of the white establishment. It took almost 90 years from the founding of this nation to finally abolish slavery. And then, it took another hundred years to get some semblance of civil rights in this country. And even then, things are still not right. Black students find it harder to get into college, and to land good jobs. We even need affirmative action laws to give us a chance to bid on contracts."

The crowd gave a half-hearted "Booo" and their arms were up in the air, waving from side to side as if to say "no, no".

Abraham went on, "Dr. Martin Luther King gave us a dream, that all men would live in harmony and truly be equal. It is a great dream and I share that dream. I suspect that most of you also share that dream."

Cheers and applause confirmed his suspicion.

"But, until that glorious time, when all men are created equal, when the sons of former slaves and the sons of former slave owners can sit at the table of brotherhood, when nobody is judged by the color of their skin, we shall not rest to get what we deserve. We deserve recognition of our suffering and we deserve restitution for that suffering."

The crowd roared in approval. But the small percentage of non-blacks in the crowd were noticeably silent. That was to be expected.

"We will not let them", Abraham again motioned to the Capitol building behind him for emphasis, "forget who we are, what we are and why we are here. So when you see the questions about your ethnic background or your color, be proud to answer that question. We must not let people forget that we are black, that we belong to that long-suffering people who have endured unspeakable discrimination, rejection, maltreatment and worse."

More cheering and fist pumping from the crowd. He had them where he wanted them. It was a short speech but to the point. He was ready to wrap it up. "My friends, I am proud of you for who you are and what you are, I am proud that you took the time to come and hear our great line-up of speakers. I am proud that you will keep the flame of freedom burning. We have a great list of speakers here today and I am sure you will enjoy hearing what they have to say. Thank you for coming and may God and Allah bless you all."

======================

America, as many other nations, has a long history of racial challenges. The current state of affairs is particularly sad and ironic since America is also known as the melting pot of the world, the land of the free. And, while there are racist issues with many cultures, the African American has suffered the most extreme rejection as equals in this country, particularly in the South. It took many, many decades after the Civil War to get to the point where, at least legally, African Americans were considered equal and where it is illegal to discriminate against people on the basis of their race.

Yet, the reality is that there is still a strong undercurrent of rejection of the people with dark skin. Unfortunately, we will never shake off this bias and bigotry until we decide as a nation that it does NOT matter what color your skin is. The evidence that we are nowhere close to achieving that goal is in the national census, employment applications and other documents that have entries for your race and ethnic background. Now, I ask you, why do we have those questions on any form? Does this not mean that somebody cares what color you are? Why? Why? Why? If we are all equal, what is the significance of the color of my skin?

As long as somebody asks that question, there will be the interest that we differentiate ourselves by our ethnic and racial background. For many decades now, I have written on the census form and other forms that contain that question: "None of your business." We simply must erase that definition, description, interest and categorization from our collective consciousness. And we cannot do that until we stop asking those questions.

Even when I describe someone to a friend as a point of reference or to relate some story about a person to my friend, I try not to use the words "black man" or "African American" to describe the person. In stead I use other attributes of the person, such as: That man over there in the green shirt; the guy in the house three doors down from us; or whatever. I will only make reference to his skin color if there simply isn't another descriptor to identify the person.

A recent incident illustrates this point. I was trying to describe Gabby Douglas, the American Olympic gymnastics gold medal winner to someone. I decided to say: "The little black girl" as there was simply no other distinguishing characteristic to point her out. Several had black hair, their heights were too similar and hard to tell with the camera angle, they all wore the same color outfit, etc.

And then, as they announced her victory, the media had to immediately point out that she is the first African American woman to win a gold medal. I thought, what's the point of that statement? What a put-down! I mean, are African Americans such that it is hard for us to imagine that they might win a gold medal? We have to essentially say that finally one of "them" won a gold medal? This just points out to me that we still worry about someone's skin color.

Unfortunately, there are the administrators and bureaucrats among us who think they need to classify and categorize everyone for statistical purposes. We pretend that we have a need to now how many people of various ethnic and racial backgrounds are poor, or have a certain medical condition, or live in certain circumstances, or commit more crimes than anybody else, or win medals, and on and on and on. Again, I ask, why is that so important?

The answer I hear most often is that "we need to do something for those people;" things like special treatment, minimum quotas, special care or medical access, etc. etc. Well, if we are all supposed to be equal, then why does any group deserve special treatment? To make up for past hard times and discrimination? I realize that past practices have made it difficult for certain ethnic groups to get access to the best education, to live in "nice" neighborhoods, to be treated as equals. But this situation will simply not go away until we, internally, in our heart of hearts, stop the separation of people by categorizing them and identifying them by their ethnicity.

I remember when I first came to this country as a 13-year old, meeting people of various backgrounds, including African Americans. I had no idea at first that "these people" were "different". They had as many feet and hands and eyes as I had, and they had this interesting, beautiful skin tone that was strange to me. It wasn't until I had been in this country for a while that I sensed that they were different. It was still a mystery to me what that difference was.

The sad thing is that over time, I became more and more conscious of that difference. Even now, I have to check myself from time to time in thinking about and dealing with black, hispanic, asian, arabic, etc. people. When I realize that my own thoughts are not right, I chide myself and am internally embarrassed that I strayed from my mantra that the color does not matter. It's hard to overcome because it is constantly drummed into our ears and eyes. The newspapers and TV are full of the statistics that people find so important.

Through history classes and general chit chat of people around me, it came to me that this country had a collective hypocrisy when it came to the subject of "all men are created equal."

So, my point is, we simply have to do what it takes to stop identifying and categorizing people according to their color, race and ethnic background. Until we stop bringing this so-called difference into our daily consciousness racism will not go away in this country; not even in another 200 years.

When I see interracial couples, I celebrate inwardly that there is a pair of people who do not care what color another person is. That is truly awesome and I salute all people who take a step towards wiping out the distinctions that we set up as barriers to true equality of people.

One of my favorite speeches is Dr. Martin Luther King, Jr.'s "I Have a Dream" speech. Just in case you missed it, therein Dr. King stated:

> "I have a dream that one day this nation will rise up and live out the true meaning of its creed: "We hold these truths to be self-evident, that all men are created equal."
>
> I have a dream that one day on the red hills of Georgia, the sons of former slaves and the sons of former slave owners will be able to sit down together at the table of brotherhood.
>
> I have a dream that one day even the state of Mississippi, a state sweltering with the heat of injustice, sweltering with the heat of oppression, will be transformed into an oasis of freedom and justice.
>
> I have a dream that my four little children will one day live in a nation where they will not be

judged by the color of their skin but by the content of their character."

In that same speech, back in 1963, Dr. King made reference to the injustices of the time. Here is what he said back then:

"There are those who are asking the devotees of civil rights, 'When will you be satisfied?' We can never be satisfied as long as the Negro is the victim of the unspeakable horrors of police brutality. We can never be satisfied as long as our bodies, heavy with the fatigue of travel, cannot gain lodging in the motels of the highways and the hotels of the cities. We cannot be satisfied as long as the negro's basic mobility is from a smaller ghetto to a larger one. We can never be satisfied as long as our children are stripped of their self-hood and robbed of their dignity by signs stating: 'For Whites Only.' We cannot be satisfied as long as a Negro in Mississippi cannot vote and a Negro in New York believes he has nothing for which to vote. No, no, we are not satisfied, and we will not be satisfied until 'justice rolls down like waters, and righteousness like a mighty stream.' "

Many of those injustices have been eliminated, as far as I can see. Just for example, hotels are accessible to people of all backgrounds, we don't see "For Whites Only" signs any more, black people are accepted in most neighborhoods, black people are hired for jobs along with white people. And yet, even another half century since Dr. King's famous speech, there are strong undercurrents of discrimination.

A couple of years ago, my dear friend and soul mate, who is African American, and I were returning home from ushering at the Pasadena Playhouse. He was driving in his Cadillac and we were both dressed in our tuxedos, looking very sharp. As we neared our upscale neighborhood, he was stopped by a policeman for supposedly running a stop sign. In reality, he did come to a stop, even if it was a short one. What really got my blood boiling, though, was the first question from the officer after he asked for my friend's license and registration was: "Have you ever been arrested?" I was absolutely floored that the officer would ask that question. While I don't get stopped by the police every day, I have, on occasion been stopped, but never once have I been asked such a question.

My friend and I decided we would fight the traffic ticket in court and I was getting ready to read that officer the riot act in court for making that statement. I considered that to be racial profiling and I wasn't going to stand for that, not in my city. I was fuming for weeks until the court date. As it turned out, the officer didn't show up and the case was dismissed; I never got a chance to make an issue of it in court.

Having said this, I must add that there is one reason to identify people by their race or ethnic background. That is to celebrate our cultural differences. And, this goes way beyond African Americans. America is this wonderful melting pot. People of various cultures tend to come here and they bring with them the culture of their homeland. Be that African music and dance, Hispanic salsa and lively partying, colorful costumes and various recipes of other nations, it is all good and exciting and wonderful. I still remember my first months in this country at age 13. We lived on a city block in Brooklyn with more than a dozen other children around my age. In retrospect, I called that the United Nations of Brooklyn. We had kids from Ireland, Poland, Germany, Italy, Greece and elsewhere I can't remember. We got along fantastically. There was no sign of any discrimination; we were one brotherhood. And, I am convinced that if there had been black children on our block, they would have been an integral part of that brotherhood. Attending parties of my various friends and partaking of their cultural "rituals" was a treat that I will always remember.

Dr. King said it first, but I too have that dream, that someday we will not care what color we are but truly treat each other as our Founding Fathers intended: truly equal. I have a dream that you will join me in responding to questionnaires about ethnicity: "None of your business," because it's irrelevant.

Sex

Part One: Age

Rudy had his eye on her. She was so beautiful with that voluptuous face, full lips, bright blue eyes, long shiny hair that hung down almost to her hips. And as usual, she wore a tight clinging white blouse with short sleeves and denim hot pants that barely revealed her butt cheeks. Sally, he had learned her name by eavesdropping as she and her friends stood at the corner waiting for the light to change, was in her second year at Alta Monte Junior High School, here in the suburb of Los Angeles. So, she was probably fourteen or fifteen years old.

Rudy had become obsessed with her the moment he first noticed her several months ago. Ever since, he had hung around the area so that he could watch her. His fantasies kept expanding as he visualized what he would do with her if he ever got her alone.

One thing he could not figure out is why parents let their kids go out looking like sex bombs at such a young age, especially since the age of consent was 18. But, he was glad they did. Rudy had been trying to figure out how he could entice Sally to take a ride with him. His Mercedes AMG was sure to be a hit with her. He could just see the two of them, racing up the mountain road with the top down, her hair blowing forward in the back draft as the car took the turns easily. He had a cabin up at the lake with a couple of acres of land. It provided plenty of privacy.

The light changed and Sally and her friends walked on across the street. Rudy said a silent "bye, bye, babe, until next time."

Later that night, he began to plot in earnest how he might engage Sally in a casual conversation. She and her friends often hung out at the mall across from the school. He would go there and hope to find them hanging out in the food court. Hopefully, a moment would arise when her friends were all busy buying snacks or hot dogs or pizza while Sally stayed behind guarding their table. A plan for a conversation materialized in his head.

He couldn't sleep that night as his fantasies took hold of him. He started to play with himself, dreaming of wild escapades with Sally up in his cabin. He had this picture of her body, with those Nubian breasts and the tight butt cheeks, a very adult smile on her face. It didn't take long for him to find that ultimate release as he was breathing hard. His hand jerked up and down as he thrust his hips in ecstasy, spilling his seed over his belly. It was a load much larger than usual, he noticed with pride as a smile spread over his face.

Although he was spent and his sexual desire had waned, he was nonetheless determined to put his plan into action at the next opportunity.

The following day, Rudy timed his arrival at the school to see the students spilling out of the building. He had his top down as he idled by the curb, pretending to pick someone up. To his relief and growing excitement, he spotted Sally with just two of her regular friends. He could overhear them as they planned to visit the mall.

Rudy pretended that whoever he was waiting for didn't show up and he drove around the corner, heading for the mall parking lot. He put the top up, locked his car and casually walked into the mall. He did some window shopping, trying to look like a regular shopper, but he couldn't concentrate. Thinking about the intended encounter, he got mixed feelings of anxiety and hot flashes. He hoped he wasn't blushing to betray his guilt.

After about ten minutes of hanging out, he caught sight of Sally and her two friends. Two was better than six and Rudy hoped that they wouldn't be meeting more friends here in the mall. He watched as they approached the food court and settled on a table in the center. Casually, Rudy sidled over to the table next to theirs and seated himself at right angles to their table so that he wouldn't be looking straight at them.

"Hey, Lisa, would you please get me a slice of pizza and a diet Coke," Sally asked one of her friends, "I'll watch the table for us."

Rudy's heart began to pound as his plan was playing out perfectly so far. Lisa and their third friend went to join the line at the food counters. There was a reasonable line and Rudy was hopeful that he would have sufficient time to chat with Sally.

It was now or never, he concluded. "Hi, Sally, I just love that hair of yours," he said, barely being able to get the words out.

Sally spun around to face him, "Pardon me? How do you know my name? Do we know each other?"

"Sorry, to be so forward, but I had heard your friends call you that. I don't think that we ever met. I'm sure I would have remembered you if we did. You look like the proverbial million dollars," he said with a big smile on his face.

Sally was a bit suspicious of this guy, but she didn't feel threatened here in the mall with so many people about. And he did have a great face, not to mention his body. She took a quick glance at the lines and found that her friends would be a while before they got back to the table. "Well, thanks for the compliment, Mr.   Now that you know my name, what's yours?

"I'm Rhett", he lied, not wanting to use his real name, but keeping the first initial the same, in case she noticed any monograms on is stuff. "Nice to meet you. To be honest, I have seen you several times before, at the school curbside. Seems my timing is pretty consistent as I return to my office and you kids get out of school. I have to say that you are one beautiful woman. Don't get me wrong, I'm not some kind of cougar hawk, looking to hit on you. Besides you are way to young to mess with," he said in his conspiratorial smile.

She smiled back, "I see.   And thanks for the compliment." She assessed Rudy with a look that was well beyond her tender years. *Hmmmm, this guy is a definite looker, nice face, well groomed, great smile and absolutely sensuous eyes. I could go for a tumble with this one. He's certainly more mature than Danny and his skin tone speaks of days at the beach, or maybe on the golf course, though beach seems more like it.*

"So, tell me, Rhett, where do you get that good looking tan? I bet it's on the beach"

"I do love the beach but don't get to spend much time there. I have a cabin up in the mountains on Big Bear Lake. It's very private and I get to sunbathe there."

Sally put on her naughtiest smile and asked, "Does that tan go places where the sun doesn't normally shine?"

Rudy wasn't sure that he heard right. He started to blush, which is the last thing he wanted to do.

"Aha, I guessed right, Mr. Suntan, didn't I?"   Sally asked triumphantly. She glanced at the line and saw that her friends were probably about 3-5 minutes from coming back to the table.

"A young lady shouldn't ask such intimate questions," is all he could say. "But, just in case you're interested, we could talk some more about it when it's convenient," he volunteered, hoping for an affirmative answer.

Sally pursed her lips and said, "Why not, you seem like a nice guy. We could go for a Starbucks or something after school some day. How do I get a hold of you?"

Rudy was in a quandary with this. He could hardly breathe, this was so easy, he couldn't believe his luck. But what phone number should he give her. In stead he gave her one of his spare e-mail addresses, one of those anonymous ones that can't be traced back to him. He said, "E-mail is best for now, my phone is used too much for business and it would be awkward taking your call. Let's make a date after school when your friends aren't around."

Sally licked her lips and smiled, "OK, I'll e-mail you. time's up for now, here come my friends. Nice to meet you, Rhett."

Sally couldn't believe that she just made a date with a guy that's probably at lest ten years her senior, maybe more. But she was in a hot mood, something about the guy turned her on. She wasn't sure whether it was his great looking body and face or that cute way he blushed when she asked about his tan line. In any case it was exciting to think about going out with a mature guy.

Rudy couldn't believe that he just made a date with a girl twelve years his junior. This was too easy. *Oh well, I'll believe it when I pick her up after school.* This was going to be a tough couple off days, or even weeks. God knows when and if Sally would e-mail him.

The days went by, one turned into two, two became three and three became four. On the fifth day, he saw an e-mail message that came from an unfamiliar sender but the topic said "About that tan line :)"

He opened the message and read: "Meet me in the mall parking lot, in front of The Gap tomorrow after school. What kind of car are you driving? Sally"

Rudy's heart rate jumped up to what seemed double time as he read the message. He hit the Reply button, verified that his return address was the correct one and entered the following: "Cool, I'll be there. Driving a Mercedes AMG, metallic medium dark blue. Rhett." and hit the Send button.

That day just dragged on for ever, it seemed. Later at night in his bed, Rudy was struggling to keep his hands off himself. He didn't want to spend himself. But then he considered, *What am I thinking? We're not going to jump into bed tomorrow. It's just a coffee break to chat some more.* But he decided to try to watch a movie to keep his mind off Sally. It didn't work; her naked body swam before his eyes. She was so mature for a fifteen year old. She seemed so in control of herself. He suspected that she knew exactly what she had to offer. *Man, kids do grow up a lot faster these days than when I was a teen. At fifteen I just barely got an idea what sex was all about, and that wasn't all that long ago.*

Rudy managed to control himself and he got up the next morning, had his breakfast and decided to do some work on his computer. He had fallen behind on his research into the history of ivory hunting in Africa. After lunch, he drove to the mall to do some shopping and at 2:00 pm he was back in his car in front of The Gap. He had parked so that he could watch Sally's approach as she came from her school. Around 2:30, he saw that the students were coming out of school and streaming in all directions. He got all excited now, flush with anticipation as he scanned the crowd for Sally. She was nowhere in sight. *Maybe she's lingering behind so as not to be spotted meeting him,* Rudy thought. *Hmmm I sure hope nothing came up and that she's not coming.* He continued to sit there in his car with the top down. Then it occurred to him that it would be better to have the top up so that it wasn't so obvious to observers that he had Sally in his car. He pushed the button that would raise the top and then he felt a pair of hands over his eyes.

"No so fast, Buddy, let me get in first." It was Sally. She had come up from behind him where he didn't see her.

"Ah, there you are. Wow, it's good to see you."

She was wearing her usual denim hot pants, this time with a royal blue top, tight as usual. That color looked great on her. The blue set off nicely from her blond hair, fair skin and the ruby red lips added just the right touch of pizzaz to finish the picture. And of course her smile didn't hurt either. Rudy continued to be amazed that this was a 15 year old girl. After she had climbed into the passenger seat, he continued to raise the top.

"By the way," he asked, "just wondering how old are you, if you don't mind me asking?"

"Why do you want to know? Afraid to be messing around with a minor?" she asked with that conspiratorial grin. "Don't worry, I won't rat on you. And besides, we haven't done anything illegal, yet? Anyway, to answer your question, I just turned 14."

Rudy gulped, *Yikes, she's even younger than he thought.*

"You must have skipped a grade to be only 14."

"Nah, it's just the age break, you know where my birthday fell on such a date that I wound up entering school younger than most of my classmates."

Rudy started up the car and said, "So, you want to go and get some Starbucks?"

"Sounds good."

"Tell you what, rather than go to the one across the street, let's go to the one at Richardson and Gussy. Less likely to have prying eyes around."

"OK"

When they got there, she ordered a latte and he ordered his favorite drink, the Moca Frappuccino.

When their drinks arrived, Sally said, "Let's go sit in the car."

Now, the AMG is not exactly designed to let you get cozy with your girlfriend. It was bucket seats with a console in between. He thought maybe that's why she wanted to sit in the car. But then, in the middle of a Starbucks, whether inside or out on the patio, was no place to get cozy either.

They nursed their drinks for a few moments and then Rudy said, "Sally, I have to admit, I am amazed at how mature you are at your age."

"I guess it comes with the age of technology. My uncle used to chide that I developed due to the hormones in cow's milk. That may account for the physical part, but the mental part comes from the internet. By the time my mother wanted to explain the birds and the bees to me, I told her 'you can save it mom, I know all about it.' She got all flustered and didn't know what to say. It was a riot to watch, but I controlled myself and just stayed calm.

"Heck, I've seen enough pictures to describe dozens of positions and actions that people do to each other."

Rudy's heart started to race as his imagination went into overdrive again. This was simply too good to be true.

"Well, then there won't be much I can teach you, it seems," Rudy said.

"Seeing pictures and doing it are completely different, though. Just because I've see porn on the net doesn't mean I've done any of that."

"Ever have any fantasies about that stuff? You ever wonder what it would be like to actually do some of that stuff?"

"Of course! It doesn't take much imagination. And what about you Rhett, do you have fantasies?"

Rudy coughed to clear his throat and then said, "To be honest, I do have fantasies. Once I had noticed you at the school, I've had fantasies about the two of us."

"Just the two of us?" she teased.

"For now," he countered, with a big grin. He took another sip from his frappuccino and continued, "But seriously, I would love to take you up to my cabin on the lake and spend a weekend. But I can't imagine how you would manage to escape from your parents for a weekend, or even one overnight."

"My parents are no problem. They travel a lot and are

willing to leave me home alone. They call my cell to check up on me, but that's no problem either. They started trusting me to take care of myself about a year ago, just after I turned 13. We'll have to do it when they are out of town. Don't know what their schedule is, so it may take some weeks to make this happen."

"Let's hope it's sooner rather than later then. I'm really looking forward to that weekend, Sally."

Sally had finished her latte. "Better get me home, I have a ton of work to get done. I'll let you know when an opportunity arises. It would be easier though if I could call you. You haven't given me a phone number yet." Expectantly, she opened her cell phone to enter his number. He gave her his cell phone number, but explained that he often couldn't talk as he was involved in a lot of meetings, so she'd have to be patient for him to call her back.

He said, "Why don't you give me a call right now so I can capture your number in my contacts as well. That way, I can tell if a call comes from you as well." She dialed his phone and he saved her number to his contact list. He'd add her name later.

Rudy started the car and eased out of the parking slot. Then he drove Sally to her house as she gave him directions. Turned out that she lived about half a mile from the school in one of the better neighborhoods. "Do you want me to drop you off at a corner or something?"

"Yeah, for now that's best. Don't need any useless questions about who that incredibly handsome guy was that dropped me off." Her smile again turned his knees to water.

Rudy spent the next two weeks jumping every time his cell rang, hoping it was Sally with news of her patents' travel plans. The call finally came on a Monday afternoon. "They're going out of town for the weekend, this coming one. We have all of Friday, Saturday and Sunday to ourselves. If you're still game, that is."

"If I'm still game she says. Listen to you, gorgeous. Of

course I'm still game. We can take off Friday afternoon, even though traffic will be a bit heavy, but that will give us two nights at the lake. Where do you want to meet? Near school is no good, too many eyes. At your house we might draw neighbors' eyes."

"Our neighbors won't be a problem, we have a long driveway, surrounded by trees and bushes. You can just drive up, I'll open the gate so you won't have to stop there, just give me a call just before you arrive."

"With such privacy, we could just spend the weekend at your place in stead of driving up the mountain," he volunteered.

Sally had thought of that as well but she didn't want possible interruptions from friends that might drop in unexpectedly and all sorts of other interruptions. Besides, she was excited about a cabin on the lake, a secret getaway. It added more spice to the encounter.

"I'm rather interested in seeing this cabin of yours. I love swimming in a lake and sunbathing in the nude. Speaking of which, you never did tell me how far your tan line goes."

"I'll show you on the weekend," Rudy said. "I'll plan to pick you up then at your place, say about 3:30 pm, that sound OK?"

"Cool, looking forward to it."

"OK, bye for now then."

"Bye"

Rudy was on cloud nine. His mind went into overdrive again, visualizing the whole weekend, from the moment he picked Sally up until that painful moment when he'd have to say good bye when he dropped her off.

The week seemed to drag on, yet the days went by in a blur. He could hardly concentrate on his work. On several occasions Joey asked him, "Hey, you OK Rudy? You seem to be far away; you're not yourself these last couple of days."

"Uh, yeah, yeah, I'm fine, just some stuff at the home

front that's got me distracted."

"Do I know her?" Joey inquired with a shit-eating grin on his face.

"Nothing like that," Rudy tried to look calm wanting to stop this line of questioning. "Let's get back to the issue here." He steered the conversation back to the issue they had been discussing, namely how to overcome their client's opposition to their latest ad slogan.

Eventually, Friday arrived. This was the big day. Rudy took special care with his usual fastidious grooming, wanting to make sure every hair was in place, no blemishes that he'd overlooked. He decided to shave just before leaving to pick up Sally so that his beard would be as close shaved as possible Friday afternoon.

He packed a small carry-on with the clothing, toiletries, spare sandals, phone and iPad chargers. His shaver was freshly charged so he wouldn't need to drag that charger along. He wished all the gadget companies simply adapted one plug-in interface in stead of the mess we had to deal with. USB mini, USB micro, iPad traditional, new iPad. It was enough to drive him to anger every time he had to deal with it like packing a suitcase.

He double checked his inventory, went through the house to make sure every light and faucet was off, no gas burner and coffee pot left on, all his computers put into sleep mode and that the automatic lighting sequence was set up correctly. At 3:15 he locked up and drove towards Sally's house. She had e-mailed her address. At 3:25, he called Sally, "Hi, I'm on my way, should be at the gate in about 5 minutes. How are you doing?"

"I'm great, all packed and ready to go. I'll open the gate, just drive in and I'll be at the front door."

"OK."

When he arrived at the house, the gate was wide open and he pulled in, taking furtive glances around to see if any neighbors were in sight. But, as Sally had said, it was a private setting, even out on the street. The only neighbors that might take notice were any that might happen to be in their driveway, all equally long and private, so that was unlikely. Every home here had a high wall along the street with plenty of foliage and a gate at the head of their driveways.

Sally's driveway curved gently and it took about 100 feet before he got a glance of the house. It was practically a mansion. Must have at least ten or more bedrooms. Definitely money in this family. Sally was just coming out of the front door, small suitcase in hand, as he drove up. Hot and sexy as usual. But this time she wore black, tight knit pants in stead of those incredible hot pants. He could see every curve of her bottom, her crotch and those sculptured legs. He just had to imagine away the black material of her pants and he'd have a picture of her naked body. For a top, she wore a white knit pullover with a broad loose turtle neck. It was very mature and sexy looking. *Damn, this little girl knew how to dress and how to get guys' juices flowing,* he thought. He got out of the car to help her with her suitcase.

"Hi Rhett, you're looking hot," she greeted him with that infectious smile of hers.

"Thanks, and you are looking like a million dollars, if you don't mind an old cliché. I noticed you're dressed up a bit warmer than usual."

"I figured it would be a bit cool up in the mountain. Don't worry, I packed for a full range of temperatures," she giggled as she stuck out her tongue slightly in a most provocative way.

"That's my girl," he replied.

She wasn't too keen on "being anyone's girl", but she let the remark pass without challenge.

Rudy said, "Here, let me take your suitcase, I'll put it in the trunk." He closed the trunk and went to the passenger side and opened the door for Sally.

"Oooo, that's a nice touch of chivalry I thought had gone out with the '90s or some time long ago. I found myself a gentleman. Thank you, sir," she cooed as she eased herself into the passenger seat.

The drive up the mountain was uneventful, traffic was surprisingly light for a Friday afternoon. They arrived at his cabin around 5:45 pm. It was a log cabin style home sitting on two acres and fronting Big Bear Lake. The lot was heavily wooded and the perimeter was tall rhododendrons and bougainvilleas. Sally figured the house was no more than maybe five years old. *Very nice* she thought.

Rudy took their baggage out of the trunk and went up onto the deck that surrounded the cabin. He unlocked the front door and with a bow and a flourish he invited Sally to enter. She crossed the threshold and scanned the place from one side to the other, taking in the full panorama that faced her.

To the left was a staircase that led to the upper floor. Under the staircase she saw a workspace with a desk, two computer monitors, papers and pencils, all arranged in an orderly manner. *Hmmm, an anal personality*, Sally thought. She had just learned about the so-called anal personality in Beginning Psych class. It was one of the electives she chose.

As she continued her scan of the place, towards the lakeside of the house, beyond the work area, she saw a kitchen, next to that a dining area with a grand view of the lake. To the right of the dining area was what she'd call a sitting area, with sunken floor, long 4-seat sofa and a couple of recliners, all surrounding a glass-top cocktail table. Windows that started about eighteen inches above the floor and reached to the ceiling, covered the entire lakeside of the house. Only in the kitchen did the windows not go to the floor, ending on the counter tops in stead.

On the right wall, still in the sunken sitting area, was a large fire place constructed of brown and tan stones, held in place by mortar. Tall windows flanked the fire place on both sides. The fireplace had a flagstone hearth and a thick, wooden mantle piece. A few pieces of glass, like vases and bowls, rested on the mantle piece. Amongst these was also a white statue of Michelangelo's David. She had seen his statue in books and always thought it was a rather interesting display of the masculine body. Totally naked, yet not sexy in an erotic way.

"Very nice place, Rhett. It's wide open to the outside, yet cozy. I don't know, maybe it's the privacy afforded by the landscaping outside. Anyway, I like it."

She moved over to the fireplace and admired the statue of David close up. "So, it seems you like naked men, Rhett. Is there something I should know about you that you haven't told me?" She asked with her coy smile.

"Actually, I think the human body is a beautiful thing, in both the female and the male form. That statue, which, by the way, doesn't do the original in Florence justice, is still a pretty good rendition of Michelangelo's masterpiece. I like that one because it reminds me of the trip to Florence a couple of years ago."

"Well, we'll have to see how it stacks up to the real thing. I think I'd like to see you in a pose just like that. You can hold a towel over your shoulder to simulate David's slingshot."

Rudy smiled at her and said, "We can consider that. First though, let's have something to eat."

He kept the pantry and fridge stocked year round for the occasions when he came up unexpectedly or whenever. He hated to start a visit with a shopping trip to the supermarket. So, he had a friend take care of his shopping needs on a regular basis. Stuff that wouldn't last long, even in a fridge, he phoned up to his friend, Harry, to provide on the day before he would come up. He had called Harry on Thursday and so now they were all set.

"I have a couple of steaks in the freezer; we can barbecue those. How about some fries and a salad to go with that?"

"Sounds great."

"How do you like your steak?"

"Medium rare, nice hot, dark pink in the middle, please."

"Coming up. I do have some wine in the fridge as well, but I'm not sure you should have any alcohol."

"I'm not really keen on alcohol, but for this occasion, one glass of wine would probably be nice."

Rudy realized he was taking a huge risk inviting a minor into his cabin and serving her alcohol but it probably didn't make a huge difference. If he ever got caught, he'd be locked up and tagged as a child molester anyway. So, he decided that he had crossed that threshold long ago. Might as well go all the way.

"OK, but one glass only!"

While he prepared the steaks, Sally busied herself in the kitchen preparing the salad. The fries were already in the oven.

By now, the sun was setting and their view to the East presented a golden sun-drenched panorama of water, pine lined shoreline, a few sailboats on the lake making their way back to the shore and a darkening blue sky. They sat in the dining area taking it all in. Sally was in heaven. Her family was well off and they enjoyed the comforts of life to the fullest. Yet, this special moment, at the lake, in this idyllic setting, she felt a warm glow of anticipation of the events to follow in the next two days.

Rudy also was taken in by the view, even though he'd seen it many times before. He felt his heart pounding in his chest and an urging in his groin as he anticipated the events of the next two days. He continued to marvel at this fourteen year old vixen, who had an assurance about her that went well beyond her tender years. He wanted to capture the moment on camera, but he always felt that cameras spoiled the moment they were trying to capture. So he let it go.

After dinner, he showed Sally the backyard. She saw the barbecue grill was a built-in design, just outside the kitchen, near the sliding door in the dining area. A patio with table and cushioned chairs was nearby, propane heaters were there to provide heat in the cooler weather. Off to the right, was an alcove formed by tall hedges. The kind you'd expect to see in a maze. Rudy took her over to it and showed her the Jacuzzi hot tub. The hedges were arranged so that the hot tub was surrounded on three sides but towards the lake, you could get a full panoramic view. She thought that people on the lake with binoculars might get a view of the hot tub. So she wasn't sure whether it would be a good idea to go skinny dipping in the hot tub.

Rudy was reading her mind, "Yes I go skinny dipping in here. The land is several feet above the lake and anyone on the lake can't see much looking this way, unless you stood up in the hot tub to expose yourself, kind of like the David statue," he chuckled. "And, you'll notice there is a break in the corner over there so that one can slip in here without walking around the exposed part of the hedge. That break leads to a door in the side of the house. Inside that door is a dry sauna and the inside of that leads to a bathroom.

Sally said, "Damn, you think of everything, don't' you."

"I try to visualize life as I plan the layout of my living spaces. That way, I get it closer to just right than if I built it first and then realized this or that isn't right and then try to fix it. People have told me that I have a great imagination to visualize tings."

"It's still warm out tonight. Let's jump into the hot tub before it gets too cold. I could use a good bubble massage."

"All right, let's."

He showed her to a bedroom on the second floor where she could change. He'd already brought her suitcase up there.

Sally was tempted to say, "Hey, what's with the separate bedroom," but she stopped herself. She didn't want to sound too eager to jump into bed with this hunk. They had two full days and nights so there was no need to rush things.

She put on her bikini.

Rudy retired into the master bedroom and changed into just a bathrobe. He was going to go naked right off the bat. He hoped that Sally wouldn't be upset with his forwardness, but he figured that she was the one who prompted to jump into the hot tub, right after he admitted skinny dipping. But then, on second thought, he decided to slip on a Speedo swimsuit.

======================

Are we all crazy? At least most of us? If I were an alien visiting this planet, and the U.S. in particular, I would have to question whether the general society was of a sane mind.

To begin with, there is a constant push to elevate the sex appeal of our young children. We bombard the consuming public with ads that promote beauty and sex appeal for teenagers. No wonder when I walk or drive, I see countless young girls dressed in explicit, revealing, and to be honest, very sexually attractive attire. Just yesterday I drove by a group of girls and one of them was particularly sexy looking. Upon further scrutiny, I realized to my shock that she was probably no older than 14 or 15. "Geez," I thought, "does that make me a potential pedophile, because I was turned on by a young girl?" That's a scary thought. But let's face it, the hormones kick in when triggered by sexually stimulating visions. It's the way we are built.

But here is where it really gets crazy. A while back, I saw a news item on TV that was espousing cosmetics for teenagers. Some days later, there was an item publicizing Abercrombie & Fitch Kids' latest fashion: padded bras for young children, yes, 4-10 year olds. And the topper of them all came some days after that: nursing dolls so that our tiny tots should be able to feel the reality of having their nipples sucked. I am flabbergasted. What are those parents thinking?

Think about the psychological effect of our attitudes

and behavior. In our Western culture, parents go to great length to discourage their children from premature sexual activity. They often use guilt as a tool to try to control the behavior. The result has profound effect on the minds of their children. Guilt can easily contaminate the entire self image of the individual. Quite often this also leads to the ability to function well sexually in the future. Sexual ability is more a mental process than a physical one. The brain controls muscles and the blood flow that is required for an adequate erection. Yet we continue to send mixed signals to our young children. On the one hand we entice sexual behavior through all of our media, and on the other hand we say: "No, no, not yet, you need to wait until you are married or at lease much older than you are." My alien visitor friend would be most perplexed over this irrational culture.

I am a firm believer in God and the essential Christian ethics. I also believe in a God that doesn't make mistakes. He created us in His image and He created us as we are, including our physiology. That means He has built into us the basic instincts and desires, what some will call lust. I also believe that God is neither sarcastic nor sadistic. He did not create us with these desires so that we should go through life without enjoying the response to our desires. Some theologians argue that God put these things before us so that we could build self control over our behavior. I think that the whole physiology and psychology that is built into us is way too complex just to provide the "don't touch the fruit" syndrome in order to build character.

So, this puts us in a conundrum. How do we control our desires so that we don't wind up in conflict with the law? According to the news, apparently a significant part of the population cannot suppress their desires and we arrest them as child molesters. And yet, we have parents purposely parading their tots on stage and TV as mini sex symbols.

Our society, at least Western Civilization and the majority of the rest of the "civilized" world, has put limits on what is acceptable behavior regarding sex. And that is a good thing, because not to do so would unleash potential behavior that would truly exceed reasonable limits. But, back to my alien visitor's observation, Why are we putting ourselves into this horrendously stressful situation of putting limits on acceptable behavior while at the same time placing humongous enticement for unacceptable behavior? Why do we strive so hard to make the female of our species look so enticing, even at a so-called minor age and, incomprehensibly, our tiny children, and then prohibit the behavior that it encourages? How, then can we possibly pretend to be shocked at incidents of so-called child molestation or having sex with minors? Hello? Is anybody home upstairs? There has to be a loose connection in our collective mentality to support this. Of course, one can argue for the defense of freedom of expression and freedom of business enterprise. Both defenses are used to support the marketing and display of whatever and whoever we want.

A look at our daily news shows incident after incident of child molestation. People in authority positions, such as priests, pastors, teachers, coaches, scoutmasters and mentors are accused in ever increasing numbers. I think we have merely discovered the tip of that iceberg. This goes to show that there is a significant desire for adolescent sex in our society, the laws not withstanding. Well, as my alien visitor would remark: "No wonder." I submit that such behavior is way too common to be a rare aberration.

And now, I will tread on thin ice here, because it goes against all we pretend to stand for, despite our actions. Our God has created us, as I stated before, including all our physiological functions. He has created our bodies in a fashion that they are ready for sexual intercourse at an age around 13, give or take a year or so. That is simply a biological fact. Why did God do that? Did He do it to tease us and to stress us out? To test us to see if we can suppress the desires He has built into us? Why? I don't believe that God, who loves us, would do that. I believe that the answer lies in our ancestral development. (And, by the way, if you do not believe in God or a supreme creator, if you believe in evolution without guidance in stead, it doesn't matter. In that case we were created by the evolutionary process. You can then still ask: "Why do we have sexual maturity and function at such an early age?")

A review of literature and studies by eminent authors and scientists will bring to mind that the age of consent, as it is often called, varies from culture to culture. Traditionally, across the globe, the age of consent for a sexual union was a matter for the family to decide, or a tribal custom. In most cases, this coincided with signs of puberty, menstruation for a woman and pubic hair for a man.

Some cultures, such as the French Polynesian peoples, recognize that sex is a gift from God and should be used at an age when the person matures to the point of sexual function. Children slept in the same room as their parents and were able to witness their parents while they had sex. Intercourse simulation became real penetration as soon as boys were physically able.

In the 12th century, the influential founder of Canon law in medieval Europe, Gratian, accepted age of puberty for marriage to be between 12 and 14. However, he acknowledged consent to be meaningful if the children were older than 7.

The first recorded age-of-consent law dates back about 800 years: In early 13th century England, a statute, made it a misdemeanor to "ravish" a "maiden within age," (less than 12 years of age) whether with or without her consent.

Sir Edward Coke in 17th century England "made it clear that the marriage of girls under 12 was normal, and the age at which a girl who was a wife was eligible for a dower from her husband's estate was 9. The American colonies followed the English tradition, and the law was more of a guide. For example, in 1689, Mary Hathaway of Virginia, was only 9 when she was married to William Williams.

A small number of Italian and German states set an age of consent in the 16th century at 12 years. Towards the end of the 18th century, other European countries also began to enact age of consent laws. The first French Constitution established an age of consent of 11 years in 1791, which was raised to 13 in 1863.

Portugal, Spain, Denmark and the Swiss cantons, initially set the age of consent at 10–12 years and then raised it to between 13 and 16 years in the second half of the 19th century. Historically, the English common law set the age of consent to range from 10 to 12. In the United States, by the 1880s, most states set the age of consent at 10–12, and in one state, Delaware, the age of consent was only 7.

Female reformers and advocates of social purity initiated a campaign in 1885 to petition legislators to raise the legal age of consent to at least 16, with the ultimate goal to raise the age to 18. The campaign was successful, with almost all states raised the age of consent to 16–18 by 1920.

Social and the resulting legal attitudes toward the appropriate age of consent have drifted upwards in modern times. For example, while ages from 10 to 13 were typically acceptable in Western countries during the mid-19th century, the end of the 19th century and the beginning of the 20th century were marked by changing attitudes towards sexuality and childhood, resulting in raising the ages of consent to ages generally ranging from 16 to 18.

I believe that a lot of our current mores come from a reluctance to let our children mature mentally as quickly as our bodies do. Keep in mind that not all societies share our Western mores. And to my surprise, until the latter part of the 19th Century, children in the Western nations were engaged and married at a much earlier age. The trend to give children more time to mature is relatively new.

In his book, *The Emphatic civilization,* (Penguin, NY, 200) Jeremy Rifkin points out that the concept of adolescence only emerged during the last decade of the nineteenth century and the first three decades of the twentieth century. Society started to think of childhood as extending beyond puberty, into the later teenage years. Before that, children were considered to graduate into adulthood with the onset of puberty.

Rifkin goes on to explain that work life and adult responsibilities were put off; children remained under the nurturing care of parents. During these extended childhood years, children were expected to find their identity and purpose in life. The consequences of this change have affected society's consciousness about the subject. This extended childhood also presented opportunities for children to dwell on the kind of career they would pursue as well as to extend their formal education. Consequently college attendance grew in proportion. This extended childhood also gave teenagers opportunities to search for and explore relationships with their peers and to decide what kind of mate to attract.

Yet, while we succeeded in stopping the adulthood clock, we have not stopped the biological clock. So, one might ask, why did we feel that we can suppress the biological urges for the sake of greater maturity before allowing young people to engage in sex? No doubt that the benefits of longer opportunities to develop and receive formal education have provided for vast number of increased college educated adults. And that is a good thing.

So, what are we to make of this historical perspective of when children should be allowed to consent to sexual activities? As you just saw, it is only in relatively recent times that Western societies decided to protect children to a longer age by prohibiting sexual activities with older persons. And yet, we contradict that by our very actions, such as makeup, suggestive sexy clothing, children acting out sexually suggestive motions on stage and TV, just to name a few examples.

Now, I do not have a solution to this dilemma. Options

that come to mind include shutting down the marketing efforts for sexy clothing and makeup and nursing dolls, etc. to young people, along with criminalizing parents' actions that support such marketing and purchases; placing stiff penalties on young people and children who flaunt their sexuality, e.g. impose modest dress codes; changing the age of consent to a more reasonable level, as our ancestors recognized; mitigating penalties on the older party if the younger party clearly indicates their desire to engage in sex with the older person (and, yes, don't be surprised that there are many youngsters as young as 10 years old who are wholly aware of their actions and still desire to engage in sex with adults). Of course some of these options are totally unacceptable to a majority of our society. But it seems to me that we need to do something. It just does not make sense to entice people into sex and then punish them for it.

There is also the matter of educating our children in matters of sex. The anxiety ridden "birds and bees" talk seems to be something that parents are not comfortable with. Sorry, but as a parent you have that responsibility; you owe it to your children. If you don't address this topic, then they will learn it from their peers. And you need to do it before they reach the age of 10, I would say. By that time your children's peers are likely to start educating your child without your consent or control of content. I would think that you'd prefer to be in charge of what they learn. Opening up on this topic will also give your children the comfort and courage to discuss such matters with you openly. I remember from my childhood, sex was simply a taboo subject and the prospect of talking about it with my parents was not an option. I learned from friends and trial and error.

As a parent, I would urge you to tell your children, especially the girls, that if you go out and flaunt your sexuality with hot pants, tight clothing, sexy makeup and coy smiles, you will be engaging a biological chain reaction that is as old as humankind itself. While in most animal species it is the male that does the prancing and attracting, in the human race, it is the female that does the prancing and enticing. It seems to me that when there is this sexually enticing behavior, there is an implied consent to engage. Alternately, we might have to call it a tease or a practice run. Perhaps that is what our society wants: to give our children lots of time and opportunity to practice enticing the other sex without permission to act on it.

Sex

Part 2: Homosexuality

Henry dreaded every morning when he faced another day at school. He was the victim of constant bullying. He was not a fighter and the other boys knew it. The name calling was bad enough, but the physical treatment he got was what bothered him most. He just didn't want to strike back and escalate things into a bloody battle. So far, they hadn't hurt him excessively, just enough to make him smart.

Seventh grade has been especially bad. His class had two bullies that got along quite well with each other and they combined their bullying on Henry. For several years now, since he was ten, he had known that he was different than other boys. While he and his friends had fooled around, playing with each other and stuff, he had genuine feelings for his boy friends. He never dared say anything, but he loved it when they played with each other. At night he would dream of himself and his best friend, Billy, in their secret hideaway doing things to each other that got Henry all hot and excited in his groin. Billy didn't know about these fantasies, of course. One didn't talk about that. Besides, he didn't want to be identified as a fag.

In the intervening years, things had changed though. Now that he was fourteen, his body had matured somewhat, but he had a baby face, with full lips, slightly pudgy cheeks, ruddy curly hair, and a cute pug nose. He was sure that is why the other boys were making fun of him, calling him "Fag, Queer, Cocksucker" and the like.

Of course, when it came to games and sports, he was never invited to join any of the teams. He was always left to stand on the sidelines. Roger even suggested he put on a tutu and join the cheer leaders. This created a lonely world for Henry. He couldn't hide his appearance. He didn't think that he walked all swishy or behaved in other queer ways. But somehow they knew that he was "different." And of course what made it hard to deal with, is that they were right. He was gay and nobody wanted to be associated with a gay guy.

Henry couldn't talk about it at home either. His parents didn't know that he was gay. When they asked, "How were things at school today?" he would give them the pat answer, "Fine, we did this or that today at school," hoping to end the conversation. He could tell from listening to them making remarks about homosexuality as they commented on items on TV or in the news, that they didn't like gays either. So, bringing that subject up was not an option. There really was nobody to talk to about his condition.

Things had gotten worse over the last couple of months, such that Henry was feeling desperate and more and more depressed. He used to have visions of his future, things he would do, plans he had for becoming a successful business man, and travels he would make. These things seemed more and more remote as he was constantly bullied at school and after school if they caught him in the park or at the mall. There were a couple of times in the last month where he had actually contemplated ending it all. He wondered how he could accomplish suicide. Each time, he woke up from that daydream however, and told himself, things will get better, they won't keep up the bullying forever.

But of course things didn't get better. One night in bed, after a particularly harrowing day in school, Henry got more serious about his suicide options. Roger and his bullying buddy Dave caught him alone in the boys' restroom. Roger, the bigger and stronger of the two had embraced Henry in a hold where his head was down in Roger's stomach, with his bottom sticking out behind him. Dave then pulled his pants and briefs down, stripping him to his bare bottom. "You like to get buggered, do you?" asked Roger, "Well we're gonna give you a taste of it."

While he was trapped in that strangle hold, he suddenly sensed something between his cheeks. It dawned on him that Dave was trying to stick something up his butt. He struggled as best he could, but between Roger's stranglehold and David holing him about the waist, it was no use. He could feel David pushing the dildo up his butt. It was too tight and hurt a lot. Once David got it all the way in, they let him go and ran out of the restroom, laving Henry alone in his state of undress.

So, tonight he was determined to end it all. Getting enough sleeping pills to do the job would be impossible. His parents would notice if he got prescriptions for those and surely would track his consumption. If he collected them long enough, though, pretending to take them, maybe he could save up enough to take all at once. But, how many would be enough to do the job? He'll have to do some research on the internet. His dad had a gun but he wasn't sure where he kept the ammo. There was always jumping off a bridge.

He fantasized what he would write in his suicide note. He'd have to leave one for his parents and maybe one for Billy. Writing those notes was going to be painful. Eventually Henry drifted off to sleep.

The following morning he was browsing on the internet before he went downstairs for breakfast. He'd awakened earlier than usual. He was searching for articles on sleeping pills as well as homosexuality when he stumbled across a site for the gay and lesbian center in downtown. They had several programs for young gays, including counseling. Henry thought that might be worthwhile. It was a bit awkward to get to, though. He'd have to take public transportation and make some excuse that he and Billy were going studying at Billy's house.

A week later, he got the chance to go to the Center. When he got there, he asked for the youth program counseling at the information desk. The man at the desk told him there would be a group session starting in 45 minutes, but in the mean time, he could go to the counselor's office and try his luck.

Henry found the counselor in his office and knocked.

"Hi, come on in. How can I help you," invited Joel, the counselor.

"Er, I'm not sure. I found this place on the net and thought I'd come visit, see what this place is all about."

"That might take more than a visit, my young friend. But since you wound up here, at Youth Counseling, might I venture a guess that you have some questions?"

Joel seemed like a super nice guy. He had an open face and a genuine smile that gave Henry confidence somehow that he could talk to this guy. "Well, to be honest, there are a million questions," he replied with a shy grin on his face.

"OK, shoot, I have about 30 minutes free. One thing I hope you understand is that whatever is spoken in this office stays in this office. None of what we talk about is shared with anyone else at this end. Understand?"

"Yeah, sure, that's nice."

"So, go ahead and let's pick a topic of what interests you."

Henry plunged right into it; he wasn't sure how often he could get here and he was determined to make the best of this trip. Either it would be helpful or he'd find out quick enough if it wasn't. "I have this bullying issue at school. I'm not happy there, nor after school at the park, the mall and other places you'd find my classmates."

"Ah, another bullying story. Hey, don't get me wrong, it's not like I've heard them all, but just that I do hear a lot about gay guys being bullied in school. Let me guess, you're in Junior High School, do I have that right?"

"Yeah, seventh grade."

"You see, that is an age where most of the bullying goes on. Kids of that age know enough about the subject to build on their imagination and they are still completely protective of their own feelings. It simply isn't macho to admit that you like people of the same gender. The straight truth is, however, that most guys have homosexual fantasies and it scares them. They are afraid if the truth ever came out, that most of the world would chastise them, call them fags, queers, homos, etc."

"Man, I have a tough time imagining Roger, er, that's not his real name, mind you," Henry tried to cover the true identity of his nemesis, "being interested in sex with another guy. I mean, he is Mr. Macho Supreme in school. He must be one of your exceptions."

"Could be, Henry, but I would not be surprised if it turns out that Rodger has already fooled around with other guys or has fantasies about it. In any case, this is a real problem, but we have plans to address it. It's just going to take time."

"How would you address it?"

"For one thing, we need to educate the population about the truth of the situation. For another, we are conducting strong support programs here at the Center."

"It's not easy for me to get to this place," Henry explained.

Joel was ready, "Actually, we are opening satellite centers in the surrounding suburbs so that guys like you can get to a center without difficulty. These satellite centers operate on a part time basis, using community centers as the surrounding cities allow us to use their facilities. It's a relatively new thing, but I have great hope in our outreach program."

"Cool, are any of them operating yet? Like maybe near Alta Monte?"

"Our first satellites are in the Valley and down in South County. We're planning one for Monte View, that's fairly close to Alta Monte."

"That is close to where I live. When is that gonna open?"

"Right now it looks like another six months."

"Well, that's not too far."

"Our most effective outreach at the moment, is our education program. We come and visit schools and present talks and hold discussions for the student body. Since you haven't mentioned it, I assume your school hasn't had us come visit yet."

"I don't think so, it doesn't sound like anything familiar. I'm sure that anything like that would have caught my attention."

"Let me ask you a few questions, if I may, Henry"

"Go ahead, what do you want to know?"

"Keep in mind again, this stays in this office but it will help me figure out what to do next. You are, first of all a very brave kid to come here and open up. I know that took some courage and I salute you for that. I'm wondering how many other guys, or girls, like you there are in your school?"

"Gee, I have no idea. I mean it's just not cool admitting you are gay. Guys bully me mostly, I think, because of my looks. They assume I'm gay by the way I look. I certainly never let it on that I like guys; nobody else knows about this. And I have no idea who else might be in a similar position."

"Are any other guys being bullied like you?"

"Little Willy gets a tough time from the guys, but that's because he's such a little guy. He's easy to pick on and he's like me in that he doesn't fight back."

"OK, now, you've already told me that you haven't let on to anyone else about being gay, so I assume that you don't have any friends that are gay, as far as you know."

"That's right."

"Do you parents know about your situation?"

"Heck no, they'd kill me if they found out."

"Hmmm, that's too bad. Well, look, we'll try to deal with that when the time is right. What school do you go to? I'd like to try to make arrangements to come there and do a presentation."

"Alta Monte Junior High School. How long would it take you to set that up?"

"Depends on the school and our schedule. Probably about one to two months."

"I see. OK, what can I do to help? But it has to be anonymous. I don't want to be identified with setting this up. Hope you understand."

Joel assured him, "I understand completely and don't worry, there won't be any connection between the event and you."

"Well, I feel a lot better about this. Thanks for your time. Thirty minutes is just about up so I'll let you get back to your activities. Er, one more thing, would it be alright if I had your phone number, in case I had some questions?"

"Sure," Joel said, "here's my card. Feel free to call me any time, including the middle of the night. If the phone is on, I take the calls. I want to thank you for coming in here, Henry, you're quite a guy, my hat's off to you. And one more thing, Henry, don't do anything foolish. Sometimes things seem very dark, Just remember, no matter how dark it gets, the sun ALWAYS rises again. You have a great future in front of you, I guarantee it!"

"Yeah, sure, thanks and don't worry about me. I still do have my dreams and they're gonna come true," he said with a smile on his face.

Life didn't change much in the coming weeks, but Henry seemed more resigned to just bear it. He was looking forward to the presentation Joel was setting up. So far he hadn't heard anything about it. Then, one Monday morning, he saw it on the bulletin board in the hallway. A special presentation to be delivered during assembly. The poster said that it was open to all grades, that the school schedule had been rearranged so that all grades would be able to attend the same session. It was scheduled for three weeks from now. Henry felt a surge of pride that he had been, in some small way, responsible for this.

Now he wondered how his classmates would react to it. The topic was advertised as "Social Relationships in Junior High Schools." That sounded general enough, no hint that it would address either bullying or homosexuality. Then as he scanned the rest of the poster, he noticed that it was even open to parents. Parents were encouraged to attend if they could find the time off. Well, that would eliminate his parents , they were too busy with work.

Two days later, at dinner, he noticed the mail had included a copy of the poster. Apparently the school, or maybe the Center, had mailed all the parents to let them know about this event. His dad took the poster and scanned it.

"I see they have scheduled a session to include parents at the school. Unfortunately it's during the day. But the subject sounds interesting: Social Relationships in Junior High Schools. Henry, any idea what this is about?"

"Eh, no, no I have no idea. Guys in school are all wondering what it's about. Seems like a big deal, though, since they are scheduling all the grades to attend the one session."

His dad said, "Honey, what do you think, maybe one of us should attend?"

"What's the date?"

"Friday, May 2nd"

His mom pulled out her iPhone and checked her

calendar. "Oh, sorry, Dear, but I'm out of town that day, won't be home 'til late."

"Well, I'm not sure I can make it either. I'll check my schedule at the office and see if I can arrange things so I can be there; it interests me. There's a lot of news about bullying lately and maybe this will shed some light."

Henry suddenly had butterflies in his stomach. He wasn't sure he wanted his dad to be there. Oh well, maybe his schedule will not allow him to come.

On the day of the event, Henry avoided his classmates, showing up later than usual. The hallway was almost empty and none of his regular bullies were in sight when he got to his locker. But when he opened it, a page from a gay porno magazine fell to the floor. It showed three guys doing things that Henry had only fantasized about. He bent over to pick it up and crumple it and stuffed it into his pocket. No doubt Roger had made this little deposit. Henry suddenly had a thought, wondering if Roger had fantasized about gay sex looking at that magazine. Just then, Roger turned a corner in the hallway and walked past Henry with a huge, evil grin on his face.

Henry was furious and somehow he was emboldened by today's events. He hollered after Roger, "Hey, Roger, did you have fun using that pic? I didn't notice any stains on it though."

Roger turned around and came running at Henry, a furious expression on his face. "I'm gonna make you pay for that remark, faggot."

Henry took off and got to their class just before Roger could reach him. They both entered the class as calm and cool as two cats. Henry knew he was in trouble, but it felt good to give Roger a zinger. He felt sure he had hit the mark with his taunt.

Henry raised his hand and said, "Er, excuse me, I'm sorry, but I do need to use the restroom. Sorry, was in a hurry to get here."

He slipped out and noticed Roger making a move to go as well. "Just a minute, Roger," the teacher said. "One at a time please, you can go when Henry returns."

Roger slumped back into his seat, brooding how to get Henry back. He was furious at the remark, especially since it struck close to home. He had indeed found the gay porno mag exciting. He couldn't explain it but it got him all hot and bothered. He was alone at home and couldn't help himself. He found release in the usual way, but way more rapidly than usual.

Henry had made the excuse to go to the bathroom to dump that page. He didn't want to risk being caught with it. He sat in one of the stalls and was tempted to flush it down the toilet, but he was afraid it would plug it up. So in stead, he crumpled it really tight and then wrapped it in toilet paper so that he had just an innocent looking wad of white toilet paper. He deposited that into the trash bin, pushing it way down so it wouldn't show. He then returned to the class.

Assembly hour arrived and the class convened in the auditorium. It was large enough to hold the entire student body plus many of the parents. He scanned the crowd to see if he spotted his dad. Yikes, he thought, there he is, in the back. Oh well, let the chips fall.

He noticed the principle, Social Studies teacher, gym coach and Joel on the stage. Henry felt a little flushed, feeling just a bit guilty about getting this session set up. If he hadn't gone to the Center, this probably wouldn't be taking place. But he was hopeful that Joel would have good things to say.

Principal Long got up and stood behind the podium. The general hubbub of the crowd started to dim. But to get things going, Principal Long rapped his gavel on the podium to get the crowd's attention. When things got quiet, he started: "Ladies and gentlemen, students of Alta Monte Junior High, I welcome you to a special presentation that I think will be of interest to all of you. Without any ado, I would like to introduce our speaker for today, Mr. Joel

Longby. Mr. Longby is a youth counselor with a long resume of working with youth to help them prepare for the world, and to help them with challenges they face. Mr. Longby used to be a teacher, teaching mostly world history, prior to taking on his current profession and passion of counseling youths. Please join me in putting our hands together to welcome Mr. Longby to Alta Monte."

The crowd responded with polite applause as Joel moved behind the podium.

"Parents and teachers, this presentation is primarily for you to listen to. However, this presentation is directed at the students of this school. Boys and girls, I hope that you gain something from this talk that you will carry with you the rest of your life.

"You have heard the phrase 'Nothing is as constant as change.' And so it is. Change is always around us. We see it in the technology, new products, new processes, new social media, new laws and regulations, new medicines and new explorations of this planet and the regions of space.

"And yet, some things never change. Mankind is an enduring species, even though we have been on this planet a relatively short time. Whatever humanity's history is, you are the present and the future. In your hands lie the challenges of tomorrow as well as the challenges of today. What are those challenges?

"Certainly we have the economic challenges, the environment, the direction of our government, climate effects, hunger, social injustices and political conflicts, just to mention a few. But, today I want to talk about a specific challenge that we as a society face and what we do about it. That challenge is homosexuality."

He let that one drop like a bomb and as he paused, Henry could see the uncomfortable stirring in some of the audience and the totally frozen faces on others. He took a sideways glance at Roger and found him looking down at his lap. Henry smiled to himself, *squirm you creep, I hope this makes you uncomfortable as hell.*

Joel went on. "You all have heard more and more people coming out, some of them quite prominent in the entertainment and business worlds. You are then no doubt, aware that this lifestyle is not all that uncommon. Yet, there are countless incidents of people behaving badly towards that segment of our society. In schools, in particular, a lot of bullying goes on towards boys and girls who are suspected to be gay."

Henry couldn't help himself, he took another look at Roger. Their eyes met and Henry could tell Roger had put two and two together. He was sure that Roger had figured out that he had something to do with this presentation. He gave Roger a shrug that he hoped indicated "Not me, I didn't say anything."

Joel went on, "Bullying is often a display to hide one's own fears. Those who engage in bullying want to show that they are stronger than the one they are bullying, all the while knowing that they themselves are guilty of the behavior they are bullying someone for. But be that as it may, I want to talk about something that you may not be aware of.

"The whole language regarding homosexuality is very new. The term only came into use in the late 19th Century and took hold in the early 20th Century. Prior to that, same gender sex was known to exist as far back as man can remember, probably all the way back into the prehistoric era. People back then simply didn't make any big deal about it. People were known to enjoy sex with the same gender and they were left alone to do their thing, so to speak.

When you read your history and current events, you will learn that many famous people were known to have had sex with a member of their own gender or to be publicly gay. This list includes such luminaries as Richard the Lion Hearted – King of England, actor Montgomery Clift, author of Peter Pan J. M. Barrie, T. E. Lawrence – soldier in Arabia, fashion designer Gianni Versace, composer Cole Porter, Roman

Emperors Augustus and Hadrian, economist J. M. Keynes, Aristotle, actor Rock Hudson, First Lady Eleanor Roosevelt, Walt Whitman, actor Ian McKellen, Elton John, actor Richard Chamberlain, tennis player Martina Navratilova, authors Herman Melville, Jules Verne, Truman Capote, and Thomas Mann, singer George Michael, playwright Tennessee Williams, actor Laurence Olivier, composer Igor Stravinsky, Vincent van Gogh, singer Freddie Mercury, Andy Warhol, author Virginia Woolf, composer Leonard Bernstein, painter Sandro Botticelli, actor James Dean, playwright Oscar Wilde, composer Tchaikovsky, Leonardo da Vinci, Michelangelo.

"As you can see from this list, they come from many different walks of life and from many different ages. And I'm sure that some of these names will surprise you. So, what are we to make of this?"

He let the audience think about that for a moment. When he went on, he said, "What we need to realize is that the denigration of gay people is something very new and it came about as a result of a certain segment of society taking a negative view on it and imposing their view on the rest of society. It caught on and consequently, we as a society look down on the practice of homosexuality.

"Now here is the surprising fact: Homosexuality is as common as the people on this planet. When you think about it, if you dare, if you let your true inner feelings come out, without regard or fear of what others might think, you just might realize that you are not totally heterosexual as you'd like the world to believe. And there is a reason for this. God has created all of us as we are, with our feelings and desires and our physiology. And I don't think God made a mistake. There are studies that have concluded that practically all of us are somewhere in the spectrum between heterosexuality and homosexuality. The inbetween we commonly call 'bi-sexuality' meaning those people enjoy sex with both genders.

"I am a firm believer that all of us are indeed somewhere on that spectrum but we are afraid to admit it because anything but heterosexual behavior is considered by many in our society to be abnormal. And I also think that we move along that spectrum, sometimes leaning more or totally toward the heterosexual end and sometimes toward the homosexual.

"The point I am trying to make here, is that non-heterosexual behavior is nothing new, it is nothing rare and it is quite normal. I wanted to share this with you so that you can reflect on your own on what I have said. And maybe, just maybe, you can help make this world a better place to live, where people respect each other and love each other in a brotherly way."

Henry noticed that the audience had fallen completely quiet, you could hear the proverbial pin drop. Nobody moved. He felt elated and bold. He started to clap, all by himself, and slowly the rest of the audience took up the applause. Some people started to stand up and before long the whole audience was standing, even Roger, Henry noticed.

Principal Long reclaimed the podium. "Ladies and gentlemen, students," he had to repeat it to get their attention, "Ladies and gentlemen, students, I think that was a very enlightening presentation. I want to thank Mr. Longby for coming and sharing his ideas with us. I also hope that this might give each of us a new perspective about this subject. I hope that the parents in the audience will take this as a seed for discussion in your homes. I want to thank you all for attending. Students, you may return to your next class or lunch break, as it may apply."

The audience made their way to the exit. Henry looked for his dad and found him waiting along the back wall. He made his way over to him. "Hi Dad, I didn't know you were able to break free. Glad to see you're here."

His dad said, "I felt it might be interesting and I wasn't disappointed. We need to talk, maybe after school, just you and I."

"Sure Dad, I get out at 2:30 pm. See you in front."

"OK, 'til then."

======================

Homosexuality? No such thing! What? When 10-20% of Americans are either openly or privately gay? I suspect that you've heard or seen the acronym LGBT. In case you have not, it stands for Lesbian, Gay, Bisexual and Transgender. Actually, it should be LGBTH because, as you'll see in a moment, heterosexuality is just one more sexual orientation along with the others.

From my experience and observations, I have become convinced that all human beings are what we call "bisexual", meaning we could or would be attracted by both sexes. I find it refreshingly reinforcing of this notion that so many apparent "normal" men are willing to engage in sex with another male. This includes members of all strata of society, professions, ethnic origin and economic position. If you just pay attention to the news, you will find this confirmed as well. Week after week, another "prominent" member of society is discovered to be engaging in sex with the same gender. And those are just the ones who get into the news. The other, what I would estimate, 90% who fall into that category, don't get into the news and we therefore don't hear about them.

You can conduct your own micro-study, in the privacy of your mind. But it will require you to be brave and unafraid of what your study might reveal. The next time you come across a member of your own sex that is attractive to you, would you have a fantasy about engaging in sex with that person; I mean if nobody but the two of you would ever know about it? This may be a tough one for you, my dear reader. But, I said in the Preface that this book might give you a jolt or touch your inner feelings.

My own evolution into bisexual awareness took many years. As most young and adolescent boys have done and will continue to do, my friends and I engaged in the process of satisfying our curiosity and showing bravado by fooling around with each other. It was great fun, but we were taught that it was also a big no-no. So, we suppressed it and pretended it never happened. We simply didn't talk about it, and certainly not to our parents.

I remember one incident from when I was about 10 or 11 years old. An older boy in my neighborhood introduced me to the joys of masturbation. It was of course a big secret. But it opened a whole new world of pleasurable experience to me. Some time after that, we were fooling around in my kitchen, both naked on our knees, I behind him; I think you get the picture. In the middle of that, my Grandfather opened the kitchen door and saw us. I don't think he saw any details because the kitchen table was between us and the door. But he must have figured out what was going on. He said absolutely nothing and quietly closed the door. The subject never ever came up.

What that incident showed me, is that my Grandfather not making a raucous about it and raising holy hell, prevented that incident becoming a psychological nightmare for me. In retrospect, I am ever grateful to him for how he dealt with the situation. I am convinced that he knew exactly what we were doing and that "boys will be boys."

During subsequent years, I focused only on girls and never gave homosexuality another thought. However, in high school, I fell in love (maybe a better term is lust) with another student who was one year younger than I. He had an incredibly sexual body and face. I was too shy and socially afraid to approach him and even make contact. Nothing ever came of it, but the concept of being attracted to a member of my own sex, as well as the opposite sex made an impression on me. I continued to focus on girls. They were extremely attractive to me as well.

As many of our so-called "normal" men did, I fell in love with my high school sweetheart, we courted throughout college and got married. A couple of kids and grandchildren are the joy of my life. We did all the social things like parties, theatre, vacations, church outings etc. And, like most men, I enjoyed looking at other women and formulating fantasies of sexual encounters. There never was any feeling of attraction toward men in this phase of my life. Somewhere in the second half of my 40+years marriage, I was on a cross-county drive for a job assignment when I decided to stop by an adult bookstore in Omaha. There on the front counter rack was one magazine that attracted my attention and I decided that I must buy it. It had two young males engaged in a very intimate pose.

It was that moment that reminded me how attractive men can be. I was determined not to let social mores and restrictions deny me of the pleasure of fantasizing about homosexual activity. On that trip, I built up the courage to seek out other gay men and become actively gay. At the same time, I continued to have an attraction toward sexy women. Now, one example, especially when it is myself, does not make any scientific basis. However, when you read the following treatise on human sexuality, you might realize why I fit right into the mold.

An interesting item I discovered in my research is that the term heterosexuality was initially coined to designate an abnormal, deviant behavior. It was initially defined in Merriam-Webster's New International Dictionary as a medical term for "morbid sexual passion for one of the opposite sex"; however, in 1934 in their Second Edition Unabridged it is redefined without the word "morbid" as a "manifestation of sexual passion for one of the opposite sex; normal sexuality". In other words, heterosexuality was considered abnormal by the extent of the passion a person exhibited towards the sexual act. From Wikipedia we learn that:

"Heterosexuality began this century defensively, as the publicly unsanctioned private practice of the respectable middle class, and as the publicly put-down pleasure-affirming practice of urban working-class youths, southern blacks, and Greenwich Village bohemians. But by the end of the 1920s, heterosexuality had triumphed as dominant, sanctified culture.

The discourse on heterosexuality had a protracted coming out, not completed in American popular culture until the 1920s. Only slowly was heterosexuality established as a stable sign of normal sex, yet the association of heterosexuality with perversion continued well into the twentieth century.

In the first years of the twentieth century heterosexual and homosexual were still obscure medical terms, not yet standard English. In the first 1901 edition of the "H" volume of the comprehensive Oxford English Dictionary, heterosexual and homosexual had not yet made it.

Neither had heterosexuality yet attained the status of normal. In 1901, Dorland's Medical Dictionary, published in Philadelphia, continued to define Heterosexuality as "Abnormal or perverted appetite toward the opposite sex." Dorland's heterosexuality, a new "appetite," was clearly identified with an "opposite sex" hunger. But that craving was still aberrant. The twentieth century ... gradually, heterosexuality came to refer to a normal other-sex sensuality, free of any essential tie to procreation."

So, it seems to me that during the early 20th century, our language was trying to catch up with the discoveries of studies and observations of human behavior. The behavior had been established well back in the days of cavemen but only now was being codified. Once we had a label, we could stigmatize the behavior in accordance with the moral guides of society. Some of the relevant studies and observations referred to are further discussed in the Wikipedia:

"At the beginning of the 20th century, early theoretical discussions in the field of psychoanalysis posited original bisexuality in human psychological development. Quantitative studies by Alfred Kinsey in the 1940s and Dr. Fritz Klein's sexual orientation grid in the 1980s find distributions similar to those postulated by their predecessors.

Many modern studies, most notably *Sexual Behavior in the Human Male* by Alfred Kinsey, have found that the majority of humans have had both heterosexual and homosexual experiences or sensations and are bisexual. Contemporary scientific research suggests that the majority of the human population is bisexual, adhering to a fluid sexual scale rather than a category, as Western society typically views sexual nature. He popularized the idea of a "continuum" of activity and feeling between hetero and homo poles: 'Only the human mind invents categories and tries to force facts into separated pigeon-holes. The living world is a continuum.' The hetero/homo division of persons is not nature's doing, Kinsey stresses, but society's. As sex-liberal reformer, he challenged the social and historical division of people into heterosexuals and homosexuals because he saw this person-labeling used to denigrate homosexuals.

However, social pressures influence people to adhere to morals, categories or labels rather than behave in a manner that more closely resembles their nature as suggested by this research.

Kinsey himself, along with current sex therapists, focused on the historicity and fluidity of sexual orientation. Kinsey's studies consistently found sexual orientation to be something that evolves in many directions over a person's lifetime; rarely, but not necessarily, including forming attractions to a new sex. Rarely do individuals radically reorient their sexualities rapidly—and still less do they do so volitionally—but often sexualities expand, shift, and absorb new elements over decades. For example, socially normative "age-appropriate" sexuality requires a shifting object of attraction (especially in the passage through adolescence). Contemporary queer theory, incorporating many ideas from social constructionism, tends to look at sexuality as something that has meaning only within a given historical framework. Sexuality, then, is seen as a participation in a larger social discourse and, though in some sense fluid, not as something strictly determinable by the individual.

Most sexual orientation specialists follow the

general conclusion of Alfred Kinsey regarding the sexual continuum, according to which a minority of humans are exclusively heterosexual or homosexual, and that the majority are bisexual.

I think that, as Kinsey observed above, the specific, extreme end of spectrum labeling allows society to pick one specific group for denigration. If we realized that there is a continuum, we'd have trouble picking the dividing point between the "proper" behavior and the "perverted" behavior. Kinsey also found that many males admitted to homosexual activity while considering themselves to be heterosexual. This seems to indicate that there are people who are willing to engage in homosexual activity, as long as they don't have to be labeled as a "homo."

In recent decades, a new positive gay identity has emerged in America. This happened essentially because a negative, pathological definition was torn down. Through much of this century, the medical and scientific community defined homosexuality as a sickness, deviance, sex perversion, a form of criminality, and worse. This changed significantly when the American Psychological Association officially redefined homosexuality in 1974 when it repudiated the pathological definition of homosexuality.

Michael Kimmel has written and lectured widely about ideal masculinity in American culture. Motivated in part by his own frustration with narrow definitions of masculinity, Kimmel does more than raise awareness of "homophobia." He makes a strong case that negative views of homosexuals hem all of us into gender categories that limit our emotional worlds and diminish the possibilities in all relationships, not just those involving homosexuals. In other words, the mere classification of one group creates classification of the non-group members. The extreme classifications overlook the vast continuum spectrum that likely includes the vast majority of people.

The age-old question has been whether homosexuality is genetic or a choice. My conviction is that it is both, genetic makeup and a choice. Genetically, that is biologically and psychologically, we are wired for sex. The interesting question I ask myself is: "Why is sex with either gender so attractive?" Let's face it, the physiology of men and women are different, yet we have sexual pleasure centers in more than one location in our bodies. Why? Why did God design us this way? Why can a man find pleasure in being penetrated in the anus? And why do people find pleasure in using their mouth for sexual stimulation? As I stated above, I don't think that God gave us these sexual pleasure centers in order to tease us, in order to give us an opportunity to show self-control.

The great barrier to coming to grips with (no pun intended) these sexual joys is our social upbringing and the taboos created that would make sex a dirty word. It would not surprise me that the religious establishment long ago (before Jesus' time) realized that everyone has very strong sexual drives and desires. Controlling these desires through prohibitions was/is one way to control the general population and influence its behavior. After all, if sex is a sin, we have to run to church to ask for forgiveness. Thus mother Church is perceived as the loving, forgiving presence in our lives that we can count on for succor and support. This would explain the solid grip that many, but not all, established religions hold on the restrictive doctrine of sexual function.

So, my dear reader, after reading this, you probably are either totally turned off by my viewpoints, or you are already familiar with this new awareness of our sexuality, or perhaps you are realizing that you do fit into some part of Kinsey's continuum of the sexual orientation scale. Perhaps, this has put fear into your heart because this is a new revelation to you and you are somewhat fearful of the consequences of admitting that you perhaps are not at one extreme end or the other, where the choice is restricted to either hetero or homo.

What I can offer you is my hope that you have the strength to face who you are, regardless of where you fit on the scale. It is all good. No matter where you think you are on that scale, God loves you. What I have also found is that I do not fit on one particular point on the scale, but that it changes over time and with my personal environment. We can easily go through phases.

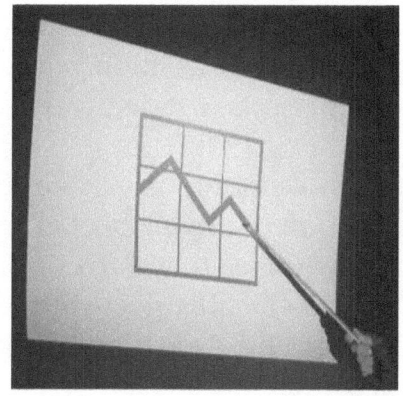

Economy

========================

While writing this book, the news was full of articles regarding how "bad" the economy was. This was the theme of the news all around the world; no part of the globe seemed to be exempt. It is a time of global economics, a world that was tied together by international trade. The political boundaries that separated countries from one another seemed to be of secondary importance. We are tied together economically.

But what is an "economy?" The main concern about the health of the economy focused on unemployment. In the United States, it averaged above 8%, which was a relatively high number of people out of work. There was general consensus that the economy would improve if we could just get the unemployment rate down.

Various schemes for accomplishing that were proposed, including: cutting taxes so businesses could invest the saved money into creating jobs; providing stimulus money to businesses for creating jobs; hiring more government employees, such as teachers, firemen and policemen; promoting large infrastructure projects, such as high speed rail systems and other transportation projects, funded in part by federal tax dollars.

Back to the question of what an economy is. I like to think of an economy simply as cash flowing from pocket to pocket. When people spend money, whether they have it or borrow it, where does that money go? Very little gets stuffed into mattresses. The recipients either spend it on something or they put it into their savings accounts. Either way, that money doesn't sit idle; it gets spent again and again and again. Think of it as a continuous river of cash flowing, as illustrated in the diagram "Money Flow" below.

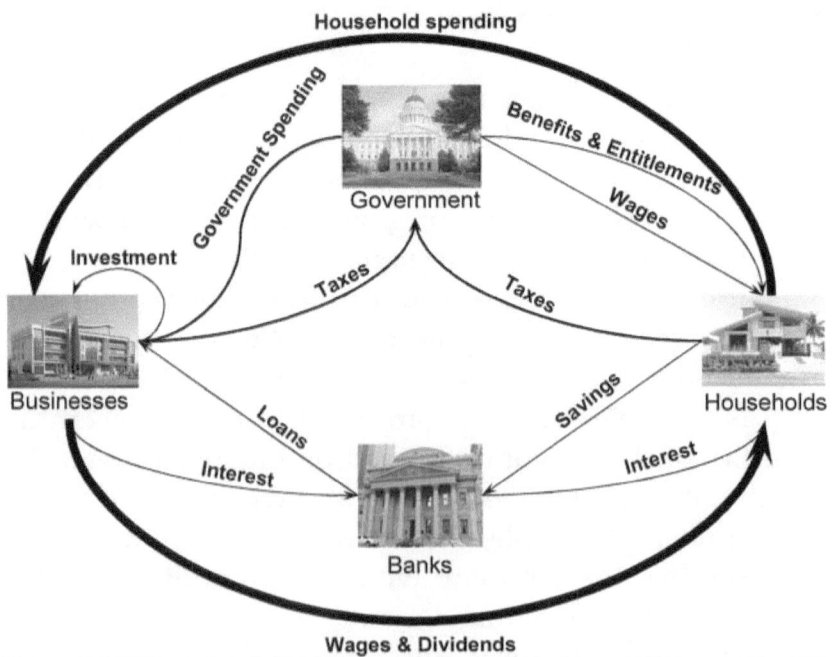

Money Flow – minimal government involvement

As you see in the diagram, there are four "players" in this economy: Households (that's you and I, the individuals of this country), Businesses, Banks and the Government. Those of us who are employed or own a business fit into two categories: households and business/government.

Businesses produce things, such as products or services that they sell. They generally employ individuals and pay them wages for their labor from the money they receive for their products or services.

Households use the wages they receive to buy products and services, and they might put some of their wages into savings accounts and investments, typically through the banks and other investment firms. For simplicity I have not shown investment firms separately; allowing the banks to represent all financial organizations.

Banks (i.e. the investment firms) use the money they receive as investments to make loans to individuals and businesses. Again, for simplicity of the diagram I have not shown the loans and interest for individuals. In essence, the banks are middlemen who funnel many small "deposits" into the required sized loans.

The Government is a special kind of business that deserves separate consideration. But in reality, it is just another business. One of the distinguishing characteristics of this business is that it gets to make all the "rules." The Government takes the money it receives in the form of taxes and fees and spends it on so-called government services. These "services" include paying wages to government employees, the defense program, business subsidies, foreign aid, the space program and the various entitlement programs, such as Social Security, Medicare and Medicaid. Notice that the Government also buys products and services from the other businesses and employs many thousands of people in the various government agencies, the so-called administrative branch of the government.

As stated above, an economy is the flow of money

around the system. Even money that is saved or invested does not sit idle. Banks use that money to fund other ventures and projects. They do not simply let it sit in their vaults to gather dust. The only money that gathers dust is the gold in Fort Knox and the Federal Reserve Bank in New York, and similar physical money deposits.

As long as we do not have excessive inflation, the more and faster the money flows, the better off will be those who are part of that money flow. That's you and I, and we spend it or save it in the bank. Note that the households do not get any money unless the people are employed by a business, including the government, own a business, or they have investments and get their money from interest, dividends and capital gains. We depend on the businesses being successful so that they can pay lots of wages to the employees and dividends to the stockholders.

Government spending on businesses is totally dependent on the number and size of government projects and federal support of projects. For example, defense spending is spending on government services and projects. The space program, until recently, had been entirely a government project. Federal support in the form of money sent to local communities for local projects, such as transportation, i.e. high speed trains, goes directly into the local economies.

When I worked for the Los Angeles MTA on their Red Line subway system, the project was paid for as follows: About $0.84 of every dollar spent on the project came from the Federal Transportation Authority and the State of California; the other $0.16 came from our local debts, such as bonds. The money that was spent on the project went into wages for the local workers, as well to businesses providing goods and materials for the project. Needless to say, the wages allowed us locals to buy gasoline, butter, movies, clothing, etc. etc. Money sent to businesses for the goods and materials went to those firms which then paid wages to their employees, i.e.

households across the country.

Unfortunately, due to a lack of understanding of economics, and the Red Line funding in particular, the local papers decried the horrible expense of the projects and clamored for them to be stopped. What they in essence said was: "Stop sending us the federal and state funds, we have enough money in our pockets." Not too long ago, Governor Christie of New Jersey did exactly that when he decided that New Jersey couldn't "afford" to spend money on the proposed transportation projects that were planned or in progress. The money was then reallocated to other states. Christie then cried "foul, we still want the money but for other purposes."

Notice in the second Money Flow diagram, the amount of government spending has increased (indicated by the bold arrows) to represent stimulus programs, such as the high speed rail projects. That means that taxes also have to be increased, assuming other services are not cut to make up for the federal money spent in this manner. A look at the government budget for any year will show that about 62% of total government outlay goes to entitlement and benefit payments, such as Social Security, Medicare, Medicaid and welfare payments as well as debt interest payment. Defense takes up about 17% of the total budget and the remaining 21% goes to various government departments and agencies. But that is a matter of the government budget, which has its own annual challenges. Just like all other businesses, the government needs to decide for what outlays to use its incomes.

Money Flow – increased government involvement

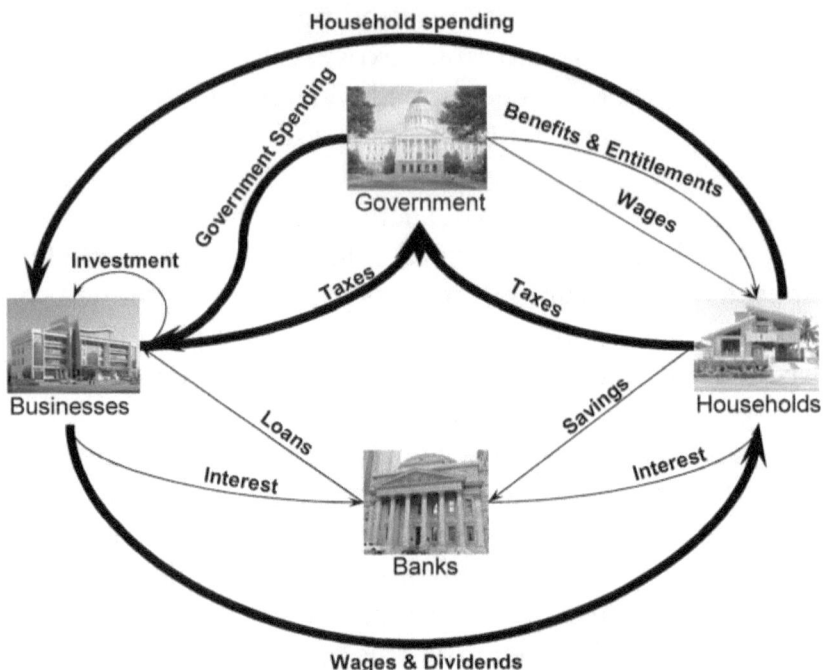

Essentially, what happens in a depressed economy is that businesses are leery of investing in the business to create more projects that will pay the wages. That's where the government may decide to step in and force the projects via taxation and government spending. It's a matter of the government saying: "Either you, the businesses, will create projects and pay wages, or we will funnel the money through the government and decide on where to spend it, thus generating wages." Keep in mind, whatever the government spends money on, it goes to someone who can then use it, whether that is an individual or a business.

Now, let us look back at the basic issue of the economy and money flow. From the above diagrams you can see that the more businesses and the government pay in the form of wages, the more money households have to spend on goods and services, which in turn rewards the businesses with sales income. As it turns out, when projects are expensive because they are big, it means more money is paid to the households. In a sense, expensive is a good thing because it causes more money to flow.

What makes this delicate balancing act so precarious, is that the government, which as I said makes the rules, tends to have trouble making the rules clear and making them stick for the long haul. All the other businesses have trouble making decisions because they don't know how the rules will change in the coming months and years.

So, what can you, as an individual, do to affect this behemoth of a system? Well, for one, you can try to understand how the system works. For another, you need to realize that this is a hugely complex system with literally millions of parts and you are just one of those parts. But, the system will work in response to our collective actions, each and every one of us. So, you can't back out of the system and complain that it is broken. For yet another, you can communicate with your representatives to express what you think needs to be done.

Especially, don't block a project or expenditure that seems to have nothing in it for you. The system is so interconnected, as I've tried to show above, that all decisions and actions affect the system as a whole and thus will have an impact on you.

For example, suppose you operate a pizza parlor. You hear about that ridiculously expensive, multi-billion dollar high speed rail project and you don't see any connection to your pizza parlor. So, you protest that the money shouldn't be spent on that. But, consider, the rail project pays wages to the workers. Now, let's consider a worker who may not like pizza and will never patronize your business. However, let's say he loves to go out to eat in regular restaurants and he spends a lot of money there; let's assume he's also a heavy tipper. The server in the restaurant loves pizza and patronizes your business. If that rail project were not going on, all those wages would be out of the local economy: no extra trips to the restaurant and big tips and less money spent by the server on pizza.

On another note, we have been experiencing this phenomenon of "outsourcing" to overseas countries. In this global economy, and with the aid of telecommunications technology and efficient global transportation facilites, American companies have been able to tap cheap labor resources in countries that have a significantly lower standard of living than we enjoy here in America.

When this first got rolling in a noticeable way, I was thinking to myself: "Oh, Oh, this is not good. We are essentially joining a global economy and that can only be bad for America. We have no way to go but down. Our standard of living will get leveled down to a common denominator." If you consider the Money Flow diagrams above, and visualize that some of the businesses are in countries with low labor costs, you will soon realize that the global money will flow into those countries and out of "rich" countries like America. This effect will simply tie all of us in the global economy to a common standard of living that is somewhere between the highest standard and the lowest.

As of this writing, some of the so-called experts on the economy are finally waking up to this effect. They are making statements that we need to stop this outsourcing and bring production back to America. The money saved on buying cheaper products and services created with cheaper labor is considerably less than the money lost on local wages. Good morning, America!

I hope that this super simplified look at the economy has helped a little bit in your understanding of what goes on. Needless to say, the real economy is way more complicated, but only in the details. There is the balancing of the budgets, that means your budget, the government's budget and the other businesses' budgets; the debts that we carry to spend money we haven't received as revenue or income yet; managing the interest on the borrowed money, just to name a few of the details.

If you think about it, borrowing and managing debts, is merely a means to "create" more money. In the end it will come out in the wash, so to speak, either because we finally pay off the debts or bring them into reasonable scale so that the interest payment is small enough to leave us money to spend on products and services, or because the borrowing got so out of hand that the interest payment leaves insufficient money to spend on products and services. When the latter happens, we get a major readjustment of the economy via recession or depression or outright collapse. But that is beyond the scope of this essay.

The Enemy Within

Carlos had a new idea. This had the potential of a great case and should be a no-brainer. The airline industry has been getting as clever as the banks by imposing fees for this and that to boost their revenues. Airport fees, fuel surcharges, baggage fees, to name a few. What this does is to keep the cost of the air fare seemingly low; after all, these fees are not advertised other than in the fine print "additional fees may apply."

The idea that came to Carlos was that the millions of frequent flyers out there have been accumulating free miles for many years. Those miles were mostly accumulated before the extra fees were instituted. So, now when a frequent flyer wants to trade in his miles for an airline ticket, he will be charged the extra fees. That in effect reduces the value of the free miles accordingly.

What he was thinking, is that he can find one frequent flyer who was willing to sue the airline for those extra fees. He can then file a class action suit by including all other frequent flyers and all the airlines with a frequent flyer program. The more he thought about it, the more he felt that this was money in the bank.

He opened up a spreadsheet and did some number crunching. Based on some quick research, he figured there were at least 14 trillion saved up miles with a rough value of about $700 billion dollars. At an average cost of $700 per ticket, there were one billion flights saved up. That represented a total value of extra fees of roughly $35 billion. Realizing that not all of them would be redeemed in the near future, it was still a sizeable recovery that he should be able to get. Assuming a mere 1% of redeemed miles in his class action, that was still $350 million, of which his firm alone would reap 30% plus expenses. The class action pool would be 10 million flights, perhaps spread over two or three million flyers. Each flyer in the pool then would reap a refund of about $60.

Carlos loved the tort system in America. It is a lawyer's dream. Pickings couldn't get any easier. The identity of the class action members was easy enough to obtain from the frequent flyer transactions logged by the airlines. And, thanks to the wonderful system we have here, Carlos didn't have to invite each plaintiff individually. They were all included automatically, even though they had an option to remove themselves from the class action. But he knew from experience that less than one percent of the plaintiffs bothered to opt out. It was easier for them to just ignore the opt-out notice and hope that they might receive a few dollars. It was no skin off their back.

Carlos decided to sleep on this and let the idea jell in his mind. But, he was humming with excitement all the rest of the day.

The next day, he asked his assistant, Luis, to do some data gathering on the frequent flyer programs of all the airlines. He was going to call some of his friends to see if any of them would be willing to pose as the lead plaintiff for the class action.

Ron, his long time high school buddy said, "Why don't

we meet and have a coffee while we discuss it?"

"Sounds good, actually, I'll buy you lunch. How about Ben's Deli today?"

"OK, see you there at 11:45."

They met at Ben's, a great jewish deli with fantastic sandwiches. The pickles were one of Carlos' favorite treats. Ron started the conversation once they were settled and had placed their order. "So, you want to start another of your tort class actions, against the airlines no less? Don't you think they're suffering enough in this economy?"

"Suffering my foot. That is just news for the investors and the general public so that they can get sympathy for their imagined plight. The fact is that they are raking in money hand over fist with their extra fees. Just consider, an average ticket runs about $700 or so and they tag a baggage fee of $35 on top of that. Forget the fuel surcharge, that pays for the extra fuel cost. So the baggage fee alone is a 5% add-on to the ticket. Hell of a profit boost, if you ask me."

"Ok, Ok, I see there is no sympathy for the airlines here. So what's your plan?"

Carlos explained his plan, "Look, I need a plaintiff who feels he's been ripped off with the baggage fee when using his frequent flyer miles. Let me ask you, when did you earn your miles?"

Ron replied, "Over the last three to four years, I guess. I mean, I fly constantly and they just add up."

"OK, so when you trade them in now for a ticket, were you expecting a ticket with no extra charges or are you perfectly willing to pay extra, just to use those miles?"

"Well, since you put it that way, I expect the free miles to be free, period. That was the implied contract. The airport fees that had been imposed for many years are something else, though. Those I would expect to pay on top of my free miles. That might shoot a hole through your theory, no?"

"I know those fees have been 'standard' for a long time. But the new ones are definitely beyond the expectations of the flyers. Keep in mind, I'm a frequent flyer myself.," he chuckled, thinking about the irony of representing himself as a member of the class action.

"So, Carlos, what do you want me to do?"

"If you're game, I'd like to have you file a suit against all the airlines that you have a frequent flyer program with. I'll file it as a class action suit, pulling in all the other frequent flyers in those programs. As far as I know, you have frequent flyer miles with at least 6 different airlines, do I have that right?"

"Yeah, Delta, United, US Air, American, Jet Blue and Air Canada."

"We might leave Air Canada out of this to keep this within the U.S. Now the next important question is which of those have you flown recently where you actually paid a baggage fee.?"

"Within the last two years, that would be United, Delta and US Air."

"That's who we can go after for now then."

Ron said, "I think what you need is a group of plaintiffs who collectively have traded in their miles for flights and paid baggage fees on all the airlines. Wouldn't that give you more clout?"

Carlos thought about that for a few moments, nodding his head at last. Just then their orders arrived and they took a moment to dive into their food. "You know," Carlos said between chewing, "you are absolutely right. To make this work properly, I can rope all the airlines into the defendant pool and thus collar all the plaintiffs who have flown those air lines' free miles. So, can I count on you as one of my star plaintiffs?"

Ron took a bit out of his hamburger and mumbled, "Sure, count me in." He shook his head and grinned, thinking his friend was on the scent again.

After lunch, Carlos returned to his office. As he passed his secretary's desk, Flo casually mentioned, that the lawyer from the Teamsters was leaving a message about every hour this morning.

Carlos biggest work load had to do with the labor unions and employers taking deductions from their members' or employees' paychecks for political contributions. He had successfully filed a class action suit against the major unions and the nation's largest 200 employers on the basis that their requests, in most cases non-voluntary, in effect disenfranchised their members and employees.

The case had been going on for about three years now and it was time to go to trial. All the t's had been crossed and the i's dotted. So he wondered what the Teamsters wanted that was so urgent.

He scanned his desk for any important action items left there by Flo and then decided to get it over with and call Rupert at the teamsters.

"Hello Rupert, this is Carlos. I hear you have a fire over there. What's up?"

Rupert had a very congenial manner, but he was as deadly as a cobra. He knew his stuff and Carlos was always on special guard when he talked with him. Rupert said, "Carlos, how're you doing? All set for court tomorrow?"

"Better than ever, on both counts," he replied with a grin on his face, even though Rupert couldn't see it. "But I'm sure that question wasn't the source of your urgency."

"Nah, you're right. The reason I wanted to speak with you is to see if we could reach a last minute settlement?"

That was an interesting development. For one of the biggest defendants to try to pull out of the case would upset things quite a bit. It would require continuances to be filed, new filings to be drawn up and everything to be rescheduled. This could set the settlement back by many months. Carlos was not pleased at that prospect.

"Carlos, you still there? Did you hear me?"

"Yeah I heard you. Just trying to see what's in it for my plaintiffs. What kind of settlement did you have in mind?"

Rupert confided that he had done the mathematics and he'd be happy to present the numbers to Carlos if he could come on over to his office.

"Rupert, I'm always open to new ideas, you know that about me," Carlos tried to hide his concern about this new wrinkle. "But in light of the late hour in this case, I'm not prepared to spend a bunch of time poring over some spreadsheet or yours to see if the numbers make sense. Why don't you give me the bottom line and I'll call you back later this afternoon?"

"Now Carlos, you know that a face to face meeting is always better to discuss important ideas and information. You can be here in 30 minutes and we can settle this whole thing within an hour."

"Sorry, Rupert, I have too many other irons in the fire, I just can't spare the time for a visit. You want to propose a settlement, I'm afraid I'll have to ask you to spill it to me now or forget it. I'm sure you understand."

"OK, you win. Teamsters are willing to settle for a $200 refund to each member of record over the period of the last three years. That's in the neighborhood of $70 million."

Carlos did a quick calculation in his own mind. With about 1.4 million members, each of whom has paid in the neighborhood of $200 per year for political contributions, for three years, that amounts to a total of $600 per member. Rupert was offering $200 per member. Obviously not a good deal. He said, "Rupert, surely you know better than to waste my time with such a puny offer. We are not even in the same city, never mind the same ballpark." If Carlos didn't respect Rupert on a professional level, he would have simply hung up the phone.

In stead he said, "Rupert, I have to get back to my other work. I appreciate your effort, but I don't think there is any common ground to talk about this further. Have good rest of the day and I'll see you in court tomorrow. Take care." He hung up.

Carlos took all the disenfranchisement case materials to his table and reviewed the key points. He then went to visit one of the firm's partners, Harry, to ask him to go over their position one last time. Harry agreed to come to Carlos' office and they settled in for another review of the proceedings. In court tomorrow, there would be three members of his firm, but Carlos was the official counsel for the plaintiffs and it would be his show. Harry and Mary would be there mostly for moral support, as well as backup consultation in case of sticky issues arising during the proceedings.

"Harry, I feel pretty confident that we have our act together. We've reviewed this many times, but I need one more run-through. I appreciate you making time for this."

"You're welcome. I'm every bit as interested as you in winning this case, as you know. So, how do you want to proceed?"

"I mostly want to run through the main argument for the plaintiffs. See if there are any holes we've overlooked."

"Go ahead, shoot."

"OK," Carlos started to explain, "The whole basis of this case is that the members and employees have been effectively disenfranchised because their payroll deductions have been either mandatory or effectively mandatory. I say effectively mandatory because of peer pressure or fear of management actions if you don't contribute. My cousin Walter has repeatedly complained to me about the way he feels at work because he doesn't want to contribute. Imagine how he feels when his boss asks him if he's contributed. That boss isn't supposed to ask such a question, but they do anyway. They figure they'll get way with it."

Harry interjected, "So how does that disenfranchise them?"

"They are giving political support to the company's or labor union's preferred candidate or proposition, which may be in conflict with their personal belief or preference. While the unions and companies can't contribute to candidates directly, they can contribute to advertising campaigns. As you know, all the messages during election campaigns are 'paid for by the Humpty Dumpty for President Committee' or some such campaign organization."

"OK, so then what?" Asked Harry.

"As a plaintiff, I want my contribution money back on the basis that it shouldn't have been taken in the first place."

"You're going to get push-back from the defense in that the contributions were actually voluntary."

"Your Honor," Carlos was role playing, "while the contributions may have been voluntary in many instances, I have several witnesses who are ready to testify that they were coerced socially or by their management attitudes to contribute."

"Are all your witnesses ready for tomorrow?" Asked Harry

"I had Flo contact each one today and she confirmed them all."

Now it was Harry's turn to role play, "You Honor, the defense stipulates that witnesses from some of the defendants in this class action proceeding hardly point to the guilt of all the defendants."

"Your Honor," Carlos countered, "Plaintiffs are prepared to present witnesses from each of the defendants."

That had been Carlos' biggest challenge in this case, getting one or more witnesses from each of the corporations and labor unions that were part of the defense. He and Flo had spent many long days and nights trying to contact them. But, they managed to line up all 237 of them. For the largest defendants he had two or more witnesses.

Harry asked how he felt about the witnesses. Carlos replied, "Good, I interviewed each of them personally and am comfortable with what they'll have to say. A couple of dozen potential witnesses we had to dismiss as their story didn't hold water for one reason or another. Flo of course processed depositions from all of them as well."

"Well, Carlos, I think you're good to go. Good job. Let's hope we can prevail in court. You know I don't like these class action suits very much, but they do bring in huge revenues for us. They are like a turkey shoot," Harry chuckled.

"Thanks, Harry. I'll wrap things up then for tomorrow and get some sleep. Want to be in top form tomorrow."

Carlos was feeling good about this case. He understood Harry's point about not liking class action suits. Harry was old school and had more old fashioned moral values than most of Carlos' younger compatriots. If it was legal, he figured, it was good business. After all, this was America, land of the entrepreneur, land of business and free market. Carlos had no qualms about considering class action suits to be simply good business, even if the lawyers took home hundreds of times the amounts each plaintiff got. In this case, for example, his firm is likely to reap $1.5 billion while each plaintiff would average $300. That was just the way things work in our system of justice. He couldn't help smiling.

=====================

Our current laws and our administration of justice keep many lawyers busy. And, of course, they need to eat also. But even at the framing of our Constitution our Founding Fathers were concerned about the lawyers.

"A Federalist" wrote in "*Antifederalist No. 1*" the following regarding his concern with lawyers:

> The Lawyers in particular, keep up an incessant declamation for its [the proposed Constitution] adoption; like greedy gudgeons they long to satiate their voracious stomachs with the golden bait. The numerous tribunals to be erected by the new plan of consolidated

empire, will find employment for ten times their present numbers; these are the LOAVES AND FISHES for which they hunger. They will probably find it suited to THEIR HABITS, if not to the HABITS OF THE PEOPLE. There may be reasons for having but few of them in the State Convention, lest THEIR INTEREST should be too strongly considered.

That Federalist realized that the new government would create cause for greater litigation. He also realized that few lawyers should be at the Constitutional Convention lest they create situations to favor the need for lawyers. And sure enough, that Federalist's fears have been realized, judging by the vast number of lawyers we have, and the disproportionately high number of lawyers in the legislature.

The jokes about lawyers are boundless and many lawyers agree with the kernel of truths that you find in there. One of my favorite is the riddle: "What do you have when you have 10,000 lawyers up to their neck in sand? Answer: Not enough sand." While I by no means recommend genocide of our legal professionals, I am a firm believer that if this country had less than half of the existing lawyers, we would be much better off as a society.

As mentioned in other parts of this assemblage of essays, the solutions that we need are not in the interest of the lawyers. Examples include: the justice system, where it is to the lawyers' benefit to drag out the legal processes; malpractice lawsuits which keep tons of lawyers employed and our tort system. As the joke goes: "An incompetent lawyer can delay a trial for months or years. A competent lawyer can delay one much longer." Sad to say, but there surely is an element of truth in this. Along similar lines is the line: "If it wasn't for lawyers, we wouldn't need them."

It goes without saying that the justice system, which guarantees each citizen a right to a fair trial, keeps many lawyers busy. This is exacerbated by the endless appeals to get an initial decision by a jury overturned. When you consider the amount of time spent on a convict on death row, for example lingering for literally decades, you can imagine the legal bill. It's good income for the lawyers.

Malpractice lawsuits are also easy pickings for lawyers. Our society has become so litigious, it's easy for lawyers to find patients who are willing to sue their doctor. According to recent studies, the average settlement for malpractice cases was $485,000 while jury awards averaged $799,000. Many cases have awards to the plaintiff in the millions. According to that study, the average time to reach a resolution to a malpractice claim is 27 ½ months after filing the claim. According to a Congressional Budget Office Report, the total direct cost to healthcare providers resulting from malpractice liability was $35 billion in 2009.

Malpractice lawsuits are filed under our tort law. According to the Wikipedia, a tort, in common law jurisdictions, is a civil wrong. Tort law deals with situations where a person's behavior has unfairly caused someone else to suffer loss or harm. A tort is not necessarily an illegal act but causes harm. The law allows anyone who is harmed to recover their loss. Tort law is different from criminal law, which deals with situations where a person's actions cause harm to society in general. A claim in tort may be brought by anyone who has suffered loss. Criminal cases tend to be brought by the state, although private prosecutions are possible.

A person who suffers a tortious injury is entitled to receive compensation for "damages", usually monetary, from the person or people responsible — or liable — for those injuries. Tort law defines what is a legal injury and, therefore, whether a person may be held liable for an injury they have caused. Legal injuries are not limited to physical injuries. They may also include emotional, economic, or reputational injuries as well as violations of privacy, property, or constitutional rights. Tort cases therefore comprise such varied topics as auto accidents, false imprisonment, defamation, product liability (for defective consumer products), copyright infringement, and environmental pollution (toxic torts), among many others.

Needless to say, we need tort law and the ability for citizens to seek redress and reparations for injuries and damages. However, our wonderful lawyers have honed their application of tort law to a fine instrument of perpetual and outrageous income. You have most likely received a letter from some law firm advising you that a class action settlement is in the works and you have been included in the pool of plaintiffs due to your using a particular retailer, working for a particular employer, or some other connection. The result is that the law firm has "hired" themselves as your lawyer in a suit that you might not even have any interest in.

The lawsuit proceeds and eventually is settled, either before or after an expensive jury trial. The settlement amount is some outrageously high value to the tune of maybe $10 per plaintiff. If the class of plaintiffs includes 10 million people, the settlement is $100 million. After lawyer fees and expenses, the remaining funds are distributed to the class members. Typically this amounts to about 50% of the settlement. The lawyers get 30% for their fee and another 20% go towards the expenses. So, the result would be: $5.00 to each plaintiff, $20 million to cover the cost of the lawsuit and the law firm pockets $30 million.

Who is the loser in this situation? It's the defendant. The business that was sued will have to pay the settlement out of their insurance fund and make it up with yet higher insurance premiums to make the insurance company whole. You know that the insurance company is not about to lose in this. They are not in the business to insure people or companies. They are in the business of investing money to make more money. The premiums will provide all the money they need for the occasional payout. That extra insurance requirement is then passed on to all the customers of the firm that got sued. That means you and I pay that bill.

Who is the winner in this situation? It's the lawyers of course. The plaintiffs are merely a tool to make this money flow happen. John Grisham covered this situation in detail in his novel *King of Torts*. It is well worth the read if you want more confirmation of how this works. Even though it's a novel, it illustrates the real world. If Grisham had used real names for the story, he could have published it as non-fiction. But, the novel format brings the reader into the minds of the lawyers in the story. It's like looking at this from inside the industry.

What irritates me is that I am included in a plaintiff class without my consent. If I do not want to participate, I have to make the effort to actively be dropped out of the class. On top of that, the lawyers get 10 million legal fees (assuming the above example) for handling a single case. The amount of extra effort to handle 10 million plaintiffs via form letters and automated mailings is negligible. What we should do, if we came to our senses, is to require that each plaintiff in a class be recruited individually rather than automatically; in other words, the plaintiffs have to opt in to be included rather than opt out to be excluded from the plaintiff pool. Also, we should reduce the lawyers' fees to 5% in stead of 30%. In the above example, they would still make $5 million.

Unfortunately, we are in the hands of the lawyers; they are the legislators and it will be a cold day in hell before they change the laws to make this more equitable. But, we, the people, can overcome this silliness by getting a ballot issue on the local elections so that the States can get pressure to prevent this in their own state. Eventually, this tort system would be restored to sensibility.

The real challenge is in order to make changes in the law we need the lawyers who are in the legislature to make those changes.

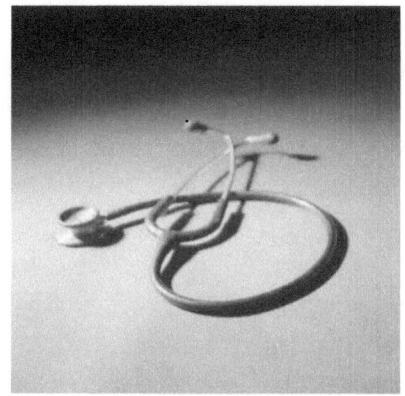

Healthcare

==========================

Our healthcare system is truly in shambles. Most people are insured for medical expenses through their jobs as an employment benefit. Many others are insured through group plans via various organizations, such as AARP, AAA and Medicare. However, going to a doctor is a challenge. You need to go to one that is in your insurance plan unless you pay higher premium. That wouldn't be too bad if the enrollment of doctors in various medical insurance plans stayed the same from year to year. But doctors are allowed to change their insurance affiliation, presumably in the pursuit of higher insurance payments for services. Over my career and retirement, I have yet to find a doctor that I could go to for more than two or three years. This was mostly caused by the nature of my career which resulted in changing employers on several occasions. New employer meant new insurance plan and different doctors.

You might ask yourself, as I have, why does this have to be so? Why can't we establish a medical insurance program similar to the automobile insurance system? There you can shop around for the best insurance program but when your car needs repair, all reputable mechanics are paid by your insurance company. If we managed our medical insurance program similarly, we could keep our doctors as long as we are satisfied, not at the whim of the doctor to move from plan to plan.

Another issue with our insurance system is the bureaucracy and paperwork. It takes seemingly forever to get a final bill. The statements keep coming in for several months with additions and insurance payments as they are recorded. It's near impossible to determine what you owe until six to seven months after treatment. I refuse to pay any hospital bill, for example, until at least six months after my treatment. If the hospital billing department calls or even threatens me, I simply tell them: "When I get two consecutive statements with the same amounts on them, then I'll figure the billing is complete and then I'll start payments."

And, if you go to a hospital, have you been able to understand and verify all the charges that appear? How can you possibly verify every band aid and every pill and every blanket and on and on that is charged to you was actually provided? The opportunity for padding the bill are huge. I suppose the attitude is: who cares, the insurance company pays.

On top of all this, we have what is called Obama Care; the notorious health insurance mandate bill that requires all Americans to obtain health insurance. We now have the government telling the people how they shall behave and what they shall buy. Wow, we have come a long way from the free America that we started with. Apparently, if an individual is discovered to not be carrying health insurance, he or she will be taxed or penalized a certain amount of money. Our illustrious Supreme Court justices have not been any help, especially as they engage in "doublethink" (remember Big Brother?). In order for the Supreme Court to consider the legality of that bill, the mandatory health insurance "incentive" had to be called a penalty, rather than a tax; the Supreme Court is not allowed to judge tax issues. But to support the legality of the bill the Court had to call it a tax so that Congress would have the power to impose it as a tax. Congress is not allowed to assess penalties.

Furthermore, the justices decided that Congress did not have the power to regulate doing nothing but it did have the power to tax people for doing nothing. In this case the "nothing" is not buying health insurance. Am I the only one who is confused? Is this the kind of people we want running our country? This is scary!

I will admit that one thing the government is doing right is the consistency established for Medicare coverage. All the insurance plans that support the supplemental Medicare coverage, are documented in identical fashion. This makes it easy to compare the plans and to determine what coverage might be missing. But even there, there is very little missing as all the plans must provide the same coverage.

Perhaps, this is where the government can be most useful in bringing our medical insurance under control. I gather that most people shy away from so-called socialized medicine. For the retired population, we have exactly that. We spend our entire working life paying the premiums for that system via the Medicare deduction from our paychecks.

So, with regard to Obama Care, we should ask ourselves this question: Is healthcare something that we consider an essential service that should be guaranteed to all individuals or is it something we should let the market forces determine? If the latter, then we need to be prepared to tell people who either can't afford to pay for it or who chose not to pay for it that that's too bad, you made a choice and you lose. I suspect that the humanity in us will opt for the former. Then we have to devise a system that is fair to all Americans. We then basically agree that health care, via insurance, is a right of all individuals. In the past, we have let the federal government deal with universal rights and to administer those rights fairly, similar to Medicare.

I think that President Obama was trying to achieve something along those lines without going full-bore socialized medicine, since that term has a bad connotation in America. But, again, if we, as a society decide that healthcare is important enough to guarantee it to all, then we must find a way to finance that decision. Typically that means all who can afford to, pay into the "system" and the relatively few who cannot afford to, are subsidized by those who can. This is similar to our income tax system. Those who can afford to pay taxes, i.e. they earn an income, pay and those who do not earn enough money don't owe any taxes.

Think of our roads. We all use them, yet some people pay nothing for their construction or maintenance; they don't pay taxes. Perhaps, with this kind of approach, Obama Care might be more palatable.

Of course we still have the challenge of finding ways to reduce the high cost of healthcare. I hear things like malpractice lawsuits, wasteful and unnecessary procedures, illegal billings as some of the causes of excessive medical costs. To the extent that these exist, we owe it to each other to root them out and stop them. That is, however, another topic that is beyond the scope of this book.

However, you, dear reader, can contact your representatives in the State and Federal governments to push for legislation to address these issues. Go ahead, get on the internet or write a letter!

Miscellaneous

This last section deals with several issues that I lump under the topic of "miscellaneous." Some of the items in this chapter address civility. By that I mean respect for each other, how we treat each other. I've broken it down into several subtopics.

Traffic

Traffic in our metropolitan areas is impossibly bad. I grew up in New York City and have spent a great part of my life in Los Angeles. The number of drivers that are out there on the roads who don't seem to have a clue about where they are and what they should do is frightening. It definitely makes a case for requiring all applicants for a driver's license to go through a driver training course. I mean some very simple essentials for safety are simply not there. The fact that we have so few accidents is that perhaps the majority of drivers are defensive and treat all other drivers as potential idiots.

The behavior I'm talking about includes just a few very basic items. These are: 1) signal BEFORE you make a change in lanes or start your turn; 2) leave enough distance between you and the car in front of you; 3) when someone intends to move ahead of you and merge into your lane, leave him or her space to do so, don't speed up to cut them off; 4) don't drive behind a car that is in the process of backing out of a parking space. If I could only collect $1 for every time I see an infraction, I'd be very wealthy indeed. If we could somehow collect $1 for every infraction and pay that to the Federal Government, we wouldn't have any budget issues.

I think I understand the reason for drivers failing to signal before they make a move; their competitive nature just can't handle letting someone else in front of them. If you signal a planned lane change, the rest of the world just might realize what your plans are and they will surely do everything in their power to thwart your plan. Competition is apparently way more important than safety. If you are the kind of driver that is afraid to signal ahead of your move, consider this please: If other drivers knew what you intended to do, they would be much more prone to be considerate and make way for you. At the least, they will be able to be prepared for your move and do what they can to avoid an accident.

With regard to leaving room in front of you on the freeways and highways, I have observed that the more room we leave, the better the traffic flows. So, I have conducted a mental study on the dynamics of traffic and am convinced that if we metered the entries and interchanges, that the extra 5 minutes or more in waiting would be more than made up for in reduced travel time. Five minutes seems like and endless time when you're waiting in your car to proceed. However, consider a 30 mile commute. With traffic at a crawl, the average speed is likely to be around 30 miles per hour, considering periods of speed-up and total stand stills. Your trip will take you one whole hour. If you could travel at the speed limit, your trip will take less than half an hour; a savings of at least 30 minutes. It doesn't take a genius to realize that a 5 or 10-minute wait to get on the freeway is well worth the 20 to 25-minute savings.

In the Los Angeles area, as elsewhere, we do have traffic meters at many on-ramps and interchanges already. They help some, but I think they need more red light time than they currently tend to have. At on-ramps this is not a huge problem as the backup can be handled by the surface streets. At interchanges it's a different matter. There is no space to wait in line other than the transition ramp. Generally, the line of cars waiting for the traffic meter extends well into the right lane(s) of the route the car is leaving. Our freeways simply need much longer exit lanes to store that "waiting" traffic.

I recently drove past an interchange that was notorious for causing back up on the route that was receiving traffic from the other freeway, both before the interchange and after it. That day, the feeding ramp had a significant red light duration on the meter and the flow on the receiving route was unimpeded, moving along at the speed limit.

My conviction is that if drivers are all moving at bumper-to-bumper mode, there is no room for drivers to maneuver between lanes. The result is that their eventual lane changing causes a slowdown and even backup in the affected lanes. In contrast, when there is space between vehicles, there is easy maneuverability for cars to change lanes without impeding the traffic. I am certain that if we could all keep from riding up the bumper ahead of us, regardless of the speed, the traffic would move faster. Getting our society to behave in such a cooperative manner is probably a fantasy that that will not be realized for a long, long time.

I'm sure we have all experienced the guy who speeds up to cut you off and prevent you from merging into his or her lane. God forbid that one more car, in addition to the millions that have already passed the spot, should be allowed in front of you. Besides being discourteous and potentially very dangerous, it is embarrassing to realize that there are so many infantile people in grown up bodies amongst us. If you are one of those drivers that races ahead to prevent your neighbor from merging into your lane ahead of you, please consider this: As I've stated before, there have been uncountable numbers of cars that are and were already ahead of you. You are not anywhere near the "head of the line." With regard to losing time, at freeway speeds, the fact that you have one more car in front of you might delay your arrival by all of one second! Multiply this by ten for the number of times you may typically cut somebody off, your behavior nets you a full ten seconds of reduced travel time. Is that a good reason to create animosity on the road?

And, my final issue with drivers is the behavior in

parking lots. Time and time again, I find some idiot driving behind my car as I'm backing out of a parking space. I do so VERY slowly for obvious reasons. Even so, I find my self in close calls too many times, just barely missing hitting a car. Of course by our current laws, I'd be at fault, never mind that backing out is a tricky and dangerous situation, especially with the limited visibility due to other parked cars. The most recent incident, and they happen almost daily, I was looking through the left outside mirror, the right outside mirror and the inside rear-view mirror, alternately and constantly scanning my entire rear. And still I almost hit some dummy who decided to slide behind me. I have trouble figuring out what people are thinking. Don't they realize a driver backing out has difficulty seeing? I can't imagine putting myself into such a hazardous situation and risk getting hit, no matter who is at fault. That is also one of the reasons I prefer to back into parking spaces so that I can pull out in greater safety. I shake my head every time I see a sign that says to park head in. It makes no sense unless the spaces are at an angle.

Customer Service

When I teach the communications module of my course, I ask the students: "Who are your customers?" The traditional response I get is my client, the people I sell things to. These are, of course, the obvious answers and rightly so. However, what I try to teach my students is that ANYONE that approaches you with a question or request is your customer. That includes people crossing the threshold of your office, people calling you on the phone, people sending you e-mails and texts and even people on the street.

OK, now that we know who our customers are, what about it. The next question I ask is: "Would you drop everything to deal with or respond to your customer?" Many students nowadays respond: "No, unless I wasn't busy." That is the sad truth we face today. We have become a self-centered society where we think that whatever you, my dear customer, could want or need can't possibly be as important as what I'm working on. Therefore I'll ask you to come back at a better time, or better yet, send me an e-mail. I've actually worked with a person who would ask me to e-mail her to make an appointment so that I can ask my question. We have thrown customer service out the window, and yet we wonder why we can't get speedy answers.

I explain to my students that there is another perspective to this. When someone comes to you or calls you, they have a need. They may be looking for an answer to something which will allow them to proceed with whatever they were working on. By your sending them away, or even requesting an e-mail, they will be kept waiting for their solution by hours and even days. Your refusal to interrupt your activity for a few seconds or minutes, is causing a major slowdown in their productivity. That is definitely not teamwork.

This leads us into the next topic, communications.

Communications

Technology is wonderful and it certainly has helped us increase our productivity, both in business and in our personal lives. Computers, the internet, smart phones and tablets are tools that help us find information far quicker than imaginable just a few decades ago. Unfortunately, it also has given us the ability to build a wall around ourselves. It has given us the ability to say to our customers: "Please come back or text me." We tweet, we text, we e-mail, but is anybody listening? We have become a nation of hyper-connected hermits, thumbs furiously tapping our devices.

The following figure illustrates the communications model on which effective communication is based.

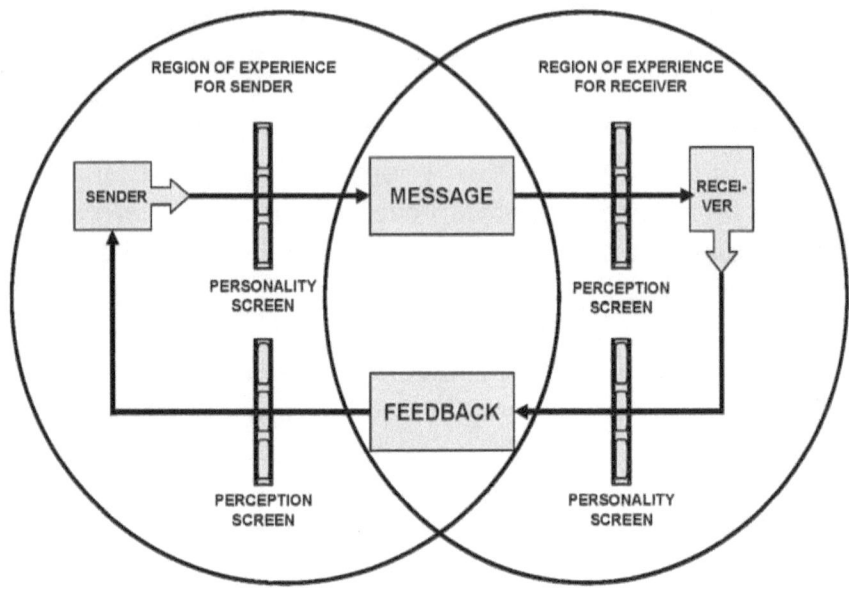

The sender encodes a message through his or her personality screen and the receiver decodes the message through his or her perception screen. Communication is not complete until the receiver has returned feedback, similarly filtered by the personality and perception screens.

Our technology that we embrace so enthusiastically has allowed us to put a big time lag between the original message and the feedback. When two people talk face to face or on the phone, the feedback is generally given immediately. With e-mail and texting, the feedback can take hours and days. In any case, it is not immediate. Furthermore, one of the primary forms of feedback on a message is totally missing: the body language and facial expression of the receiver, and the sender on receiving the feedback.

So, while technology has done a lot for us, even in communications, it has produced a major hit on effective communications, and it has allowed us to hide behind our electronic walls so that we can ignore our customers at will. The scary part is that I hear the younger generation embracing this new mode as cool, fast and effective. That is very sad and makes me wonder where it will lead in the coming decades. Perhaps eventually all human interaction will cease as we do our thing in our own private electronic bubbles.

Election Process

Under the guise of a representative democracy, the American people are actually disenfranchised. Our presidential election system is complex and not necessarily democratic. It is actually possible to be elected president without receiving the majority of the popular vote. As a refresher, how is it supposed to work and how does it work?

First, let's look at what the Constitution says on the subject, per Amendment XII, dated 1804. Each state is to establish a number of electors equal to the number of senators plus the number of representatives in the House. These electors are to vote for two people, at least one of whom is from a different state than theirs. All the electoral votes are sent to Washington, DC for counting before the Senate and House of Representatives. The person with the most votes for president is elected president and the person with the most votes for vice president is elected vice president.

Second, let's look at how it actually works. Basically it works as described in the previous paragraph, except that the States apparently have decided to unify all the electoral votes for the state and cast all electoral votes for one individual.

There is no provision in the Constitution that all of a state's electoral votes go to the individual with the majority of electoral votes. This is something the individual states have decided to do. While that may be legal in the statuary sense, it makes no sense from a democratic perspective. The people who have voted for their electors on the basis of whom they want to be president may have their vote discounted by this all or nothing policy.

It is my belief that our Founding Fathers set up this kind of system on the basis of practicality and geography, as well as the available technology. It was simply not practical to collect millions of votes spread over a vast region such as America. The electoral system was more practical, given the technology.

Considering the current technology at hand, it seems to me that it is high time to amend the Constitution so that the president and vice president are elected on the simple majority of the popular vote. There is simply no reason at all not to adopt this.

A quick analysis of the 2012 presidential election results shows that President Obama received about 60% of the electoral votes, 332 vs. 206 for Mitt Romney. Based on the popular vote, if the electoral votes had been cast as originally intended in the Constituion, as amended, the result would have been much different: Obama would have received 274 votes to Romney's 264. This wouldn't change the decision of who should be president, but it does show that President Obama has much less of the support and mandate of the American people than appears in the post election media.

My point is, with the current system, my personal vote is simply disconnected form the process. Perhaps it is time for all of us to contact our representatives and ask for a Constitutional Amendment that changes the presidential election to a popular vote format.

Campaign Financing

It is high time that we stop our system of buying election. Campaign spending is essentially unregulated and totally favors those with deep pockets. We repeatedly hear about influence buying and returning favors for campaign funds. With this situation, big business and labor unions have a huge effect on the outcome of national and local elections.

Their financial clout is simply too big compared to the "clout" of the individual voters.

It seems to me that the only way to make this fair is to level the financial playing field of candidates so that money does not matter. One way to do this is to establish a campaign fund that is fixed for each office or position. This fund could be administered by the federal government, e.g. the IRS or the US Treasury. This fund would give each candidate the same amount of money and what they do with that in their campaigning is up to them. Gone is the ability to influence votes and candidates with "favor IOUs".

I suspect that this would also limit the smear campaigns and increase the useful messages that the candidates would then be focusing; it's a better use of limited funds.

Another area of campaign funding that is unnecessary is the advertising for and against various propositions. In the last election in California, there were twelve propositions on the ballot. The pro and con ads on TV were a constant barrage of misrepresentations and outright lies. There is no need for any kind of advertising on the propositions. The voter pamphlets have the text in detail as well as summarized so that the ordinary voter can read and decide. We don't need other people's interpretations, especially when they are downright wrong. It is so bad that it is silly not to read the texts in detail and determine what is really being proposed. Why do we allow people to lie to the public? It's time to change the system.

Free Speech

In America, the concept of free speech takes on the mantle of the holy grail. It is considered absolutely sacrosanct. It is used as a defense for many actions, including those that border on the ludicrous.

One thing we seem to lose sight of is the consequences

of our speech. We may cause inadvertent harm by our words and then claim "I was just exercising my right to free speech" as a defense. Let us look at a recent example.

Producers of the film *Innocence of Muslims* quite possibly had no idea of the effect their film, which apparently mocks the Prophet Muhammad, would have on the world. They claim their right to make such a film as a matter of the American freedom of free speech. And they do indeed have a right to make such a film.

Now, don't get me wrong here, I do not condone violence, even in protest, nor support the actions of the Muslims who took advantage of the film to wreck havoc and kill. However, we cannot escape the fact that the film was offensive to the Muslim world. While we may not have any respect for what the Muslim world thinks (though I think we should and do), when we make offensive statements, even under the guise of free speech, we also need to take responsibility for the result of our speech.

If you defame a person in this country, you answer to the law and suffer the consequences.

If you call someone a liar, and that person proves you wrong, you may face charges of slander.

If you advertise falsities about a product or service, you may face charges of false advertising.

But, it seems there is no law against lying to the public. An example that comes to mind in the recent election are the falsehoods that were advertised by the proponents and opponents of the various propositions in California (I have no information about propositions in other states). I was amazed that those organizations got away with outright lies that became obvious when comparing their statements to the text of the propositions. Is that covered by the right to free speech? I don't think it should be. Lying is simply morally wrong and, as a society, we should not condone it. Use your right to free speech to lie and you should be held liable for wrongdoing.

Conclusion

If you have read all the way through to this point, you will have experienced various emotions, perhaps ranging from outrage to fear to embarrassment or even outright joy that someone besides yourself has similar feelings and ideas. I hope that as you passed through the pages dealing with our American liberties and freedom and those regarding "Big Brother", you will realize that this country is truly heading into a direction that will return us to a state of serfdom and servitude. I hope that you will be inspired to read up on our Founding Fathers, such as Thomas Pain's *Common Sense*, the *Federalist Papers* and the *Antifederalist Papers*. I trust that you will at the very least become familiar with our *Declaration of Independence* and the *Constitution of the United States*. These are the fundamental documents that define your freedom. I hope that you care to protect those, rather than continue to be lulled into subtle acceptance of the return to serfdom and servitude.

As you read the chapter on Crime Prevention and Guns, I hope you appreciated an understanding of why our Founding Fathers insisted on this right to carry arms. Today we are fairly comfortable with our government and don't seem to worry about soldiers being billeted in our homes or about searches of our homes and properties without good reason. We don't seem to think that we need to rise up in arms to throw our government people out of office forcefully. Consequently, not many people seem to think the right of the people to bear arms is important. Perhaps it isn't, but that approach definitely will put the people at the mercy of those in government. And that is how despots get into power.

Related to the right to bear arms, is the issue of how to deal with those who would use guns to commit crimes and how we can prevent gun-related crimes from happening in the first place. Do you have the strength to deal out appropriate punishment to those who would commit crimes anyway? Do you understand the connection between punishment and behavior? Do you have the courage to demand appropriate social behavior (e.g. not killing someone) via the use of punishment or do you believe that over time we can instill moral values in everybody so that nobody will even think of committing a crime? Or do you have another solution to reducing crime? Perhaps to you, the level of crime is acceptable. These are things only you can decide.

In the chapter on Separation of Church and State, we explored what the Constitution really says on this topic. I hope that you came to realize that much of the discussion on separation of Church and State is off track and not what our Founding Fathers wanted. You may feel that today, this provision is no longer appropriate to our society and that we do indeed want to prohibit ANY public display of religion or the principles of religious values, such as the Ten Commandments. Perhaps it is time to ban "LOVE JESUS" or similar bumper stickers because the car travels on public roads.

If that is the case, the Constitution made provision for changing it via an Amendment. If that is how we as Americans feel, let's use the proper process to revise our supreme law. But, I fear that the admonition given by The Fellowship of Christian Athletes is prophetic in every sense: "If we choose to remove truly positive influences such as prayer from our schools, we must no longer be perplexed when appalling tragedies become increasingly and disturbingly common."

I hope that the chapter on Race has given you a beacon of light to end racism in this country. We simply MUST stop categorizing ourselves and putting us into boxes. As long as we continue to ask: "What is your race or ethnic background?" it means that racism is important and that we must maintain it. I hope that you have the courage to join me in ignoring what color anyone's skin is and to say to those who would ask the question: "None of your business!"

In the chapters on Sex, I have touched on some raw nerves, I'm sure. I apologize if this has made you uncomfortable. I hope that you have the courage to look into your own soul and see yourself as you are, whether that is completely heterosexual, completely homosexual or somewhere in between. It is my hope that that you join me in the belief that God doesn't make mistakes and he doesn't tease us just to build character in us. That He has given us our feelings and physiological functions and desires for a purpose other than to withhold these pleasures.

With regard to the age of consent, I do not know what the answer is, but I do feel that our society is in total conflict between what we consider proper and legal and what we entice the public with via our advertising, movies, TV and games for example.

In the chapter on Economy, I have tried to give you a very high level picture of how our economy works. I hope that you can now realize that cost is not necessarily bad. When things cost something, all it means is that money is flowing. It is flowing from one hand to another and that is what an economy is. If you are a store keeper or provider of any kind of service, rejoice that things cost. It means someone is being paid that cost and now has money to buy your goods and services. Surely you must agree that is good.

Under Healthcare we explored our current dysfunctional system of providing healthcare at reasonable costs and the state of our medical insurance system. I hope you can agree that we must modify the system. The question is whether we want to funnel those costs through a government mandated process or through private enterprise via the economic system. Do we want to continue with the horror of finding a new doctor just because the doctor changed insurance plans?

If you are a lawyer, I apologize for my stance on your profession. But I hope the rest of you understand what the lawyers are doing to our society. Don't get me wrong, we do need lawyers for some purposes, such as pursuing those who do us wrong or fail to live up to their part of a contract, for example. But the challenge for our society is how to get more non-lawyers into the legislature so that the laws they pass are not totally biased in favor of the legal profession that obviously would love to increase the need for lawyers. The tort system that we currently have, which is nothing but a lawyer's guaranteed income system, needs revision as I indicated above. At the very least, when you get one of those class action letters, opt out. You may agree that the company did wrong, but do you really want to settle for $5.00 when the lawyers get $30 million?

In the chapter of Miscellaneous items I have touched on several issues that we, as a society, have allowed to become life changing trends. The lack of respect on the road, the selfishness of e-mail, voice mail and texting are a growing concern in our society. What kind of people do we want to be? Do we really want to say to our "customers" that they are not important, that we don't give a damn about their needs?

On the subjects of our election system and campaign funding, I hope you will be motivated to contact your representatives to request changes to the system. And, on the matter of free speech, I hope you will consider the effect of your "speech" on others and be willing to accept the consequences.

I hope that this journey around things that are troubling in America has piqued your interest and perhaps will stir you to take action to set things right once more. I believe in the American spirit that has always said, we can do it and liberty does matter to us.